A Transforming Heritage

Saint Mary's University
of Minnesota

1912–2012

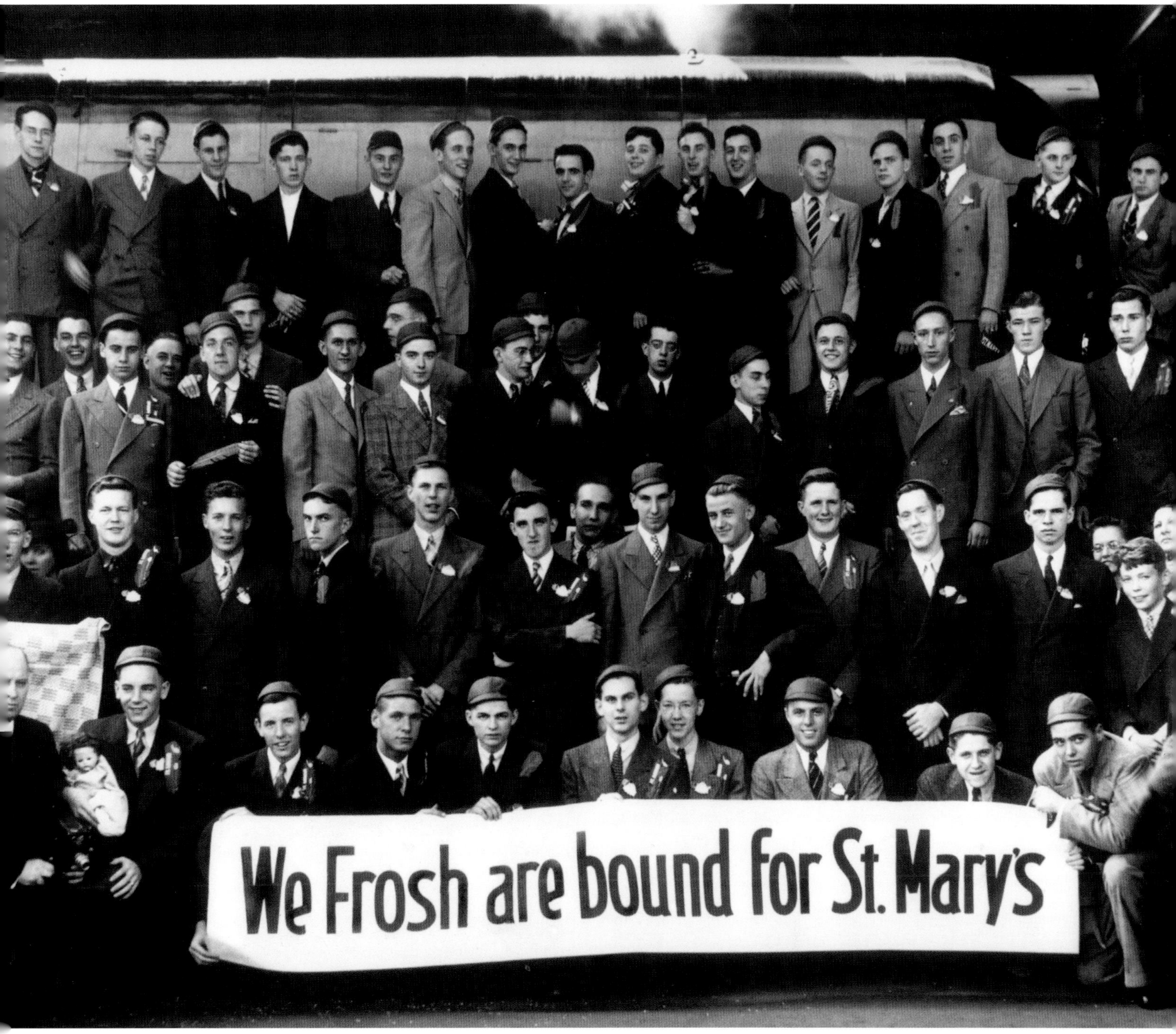

A Transforming Heritage

Saint Mary's University of Minnesota

1912–2012

By Bill Beck

Acknowledgments

Thanks to the following for their roles in the research for and review of this book:

Brother Paul Grass
University Advancement staff

Centennial Book Editorial Committee:

Donna Aronson
James Bedtke
Michael Charron
William Crozier
Don St. Dennis
Marcel Dumestre
Nicole Fennern
Michael Flanagan
Brother Lawrence Humphrey, FSC
Cynthia Marek
Ann Merchlewitz
Meg Richtman
Sister Judith Schaefer, OP
Steven Titus

Centennial Celebration Committee:

Michael Charron, Centennial Co-Chair
Steven Titus, Centennial Co-Chair
Meg Richtman, Centennial Director

Donna Aronson
Bob Conover
Brother Pat Conway, FSC
Barbara Croucher
Marilyn Frost
Tim Gossen
Linka Holey
Brother Larry Humphrey, FSC
Nick Lemmer
Judy Myers
Shannon A. Nelson
Kathy Pederson
Teresa Speck
Don St. Dennis

THE
DONNING COMPANY
PUBLISHERS

The Donning Company Publishers
184 Business Park Drive, Suite 206
Virginia Beach, VA 23462

Steve Mull, General Manager
Barbara Buchanan, Office Manager
Heather L. Floyd, Editor
Chad Harper Casey, Graphic Designer
Priscilla Odango, Imaging Artist
Lori Kennedy, Project Research Coordinator
Tonya Washam, Marketing Specialist
Pamela Engelhard, Marketing Advisor

Steve Mull, Project Director

Library of Congress Cataloging-in-Publication Data

Beck, Bill.
A transforming heritage : Saint Mary's University of Minnesota, 1912-2012 / by Bill Beck.
p. cm.
ISBN 978-1-57864-781-1 (hardcover : alk. paper)
1. Saint Mary's University of Minnesota--History. 2. St. Mary's College (Winona, Minn.)--History. I. Title.
LD4821.S871.B43 2012
378.776'12--dc23
2012032838

Printed in the United States of America at Walsworth Publishing Company

Table of Contents

Dear Friends:

It is with great joy that I invite you to explore the pages of this volume. Published on the occasion of the yearlong Centennial Celebration of Saint Mary's University, this book is sure to entertain and inspire by bringing to life many of the stories from the first century.

This book is about remembering the many people and events that have played vital roles in making Saint Mary's the institution of educational excellence that it is today.

Saint Mary's University of Minnesota was founded in 1912 by Bishop Patrick R. Heffron, the second Bishop of Winona. A pioneer in Catholic education, Bishop Heffron founded Saint Mary's to provide education for young men and boys of southern Minnesota. In the 100 years since, Saint Mary's history is punctuated by a series of transformational moments. You'll find this book arranged accordingly.

In 1933, the Brothers of the Christian Schools, which as you know is an international, Catholic teaching order founded in 17th-century France by Saint John Baptist de La Salle, purchased Saint Mary's College from the Diocese of Winona. Brother Leopold Julian Dodd, Saint Mary's first Christian Brother president, is honored during this centennial year by having the newest campus residence hall named in his honor.

Other significant times of change illustrated in this book include the evolution of Saint Mary's to a coeducational institution with the admission of women in 1969, and later the pioneering efforts in graduate education—offered first in Winona and later on campuses across the state of Minnesota and around the world.

Our rich heritage will serve as a strong foundation for our second century. The growth in this university since 1912 was perhaps unforeseen by Saint Mary's early founders. What was once a small school for young men is today is a top-tier, national university with a global footprint. The opportunities our second century holds in store for us are limitless.

We appreciate the role you have played—and continue to play—in Saint Mary's transforming heritage.

Brother William Mann, FSC
President

As you turn the pages of this commemorative book, there's no doubt you'll be amazed by the growth of Saint Mary's University of Minnesota.

The first section details the inspiring vision of Saint Mary's founders. Under the leadership of Bishop Patrick Heffron, the cornerstone for what would become a global university was laid.

Each subsequent page holds countless details about the men and women who helped to shape the university's future. From black-and-white photos of early students to vibrant color photos that depict Saint Mary's active campuses, it's fascinating to watch how the face of SMU changed from young men to men and women, and from undergraduates to graduate students of all ages.

In my opinion, the book can never be big enough. The book couldn't begin to capture the many people who have worked and studied at Saint Mary's in its 100-year history. Each one of us could write a page, or even a chapter, of our memories—of the faculty who shaped us, inspired us, and sometimes disciplined us; and of our classmates, who for four years became like family. Each corner of the Winona campus, for me, holds memories.

And, as I revisit the campus now, it's hard not to reflect on how things have changed.

Along with growth, there must be change. We are, after all, following the teachings of Saint John Baptist de La Salle, who firmly believed that educational institutions must adapt to meet the needs of learners.

But the more things change, I'm proud to say the more things stay the same. Students today still receive a quality education and people know each other by their first names. Teachers still challenge their students to think outside the box, and learning isn't just contained in a classroom. Though there are fewer Brothers than when I was a student, the Lasallian spirit still flows through the university.

With our expanding graduate programs, our presence in Nairobi and Jamaica, and our First-Generation Initiative, we're able to reach out to new communities of learners on further ends of the globe.

I hope you'll join me in feeling pride as you read about Saint Mary's transforming heritage, and I hope you'll help to inspire the university's next century. We can all say we've played a role in Saint Mary's history; now let's envision the future.

Michael Gostomski '62
Chair, Board of Trustees

Chapter 1

FOUNDING: 1912–1932

May 30, 1912, Memorial Day, was a spectacularly beautiful day in Winona. Hundreds of people from near and far attended the Decoration Day procession and 9 a.m. outdoor Mass at St. Mary's Cemetery (east of town, beyond Sugar Loaf), then the 2 p.m. cornerstone-laying at Saint Mary's College (Terrace Heights, west of town), and lastly, the 4:30 p.m. cornerstone-laying at the classroom and conservatory building under construction at the College of Saint Teresa (Broadway and Vila, midtown). Both buildings were under construction by Butler Brothers of St. Paul.

Great Western Railway trains ran every half hour between 8 a.m. and 5 p.m., with stops at St. Mary's Cemetery, Mankato Street crossing; at the foot of Center Street; and at Terrace Heights. Clergy, altar boys, choirs, schoolchildren, parishioners, Civil War and Spanish-American War veterans, farm families, city-dwellers—young and old—prayed, sang, picnicked, and heard Bishop Patrick R. Heffron give three speeches that day. The Choral Society of Cotter High School, which opened the year before and was staffed by the Christian Brothers, performed at the cemetery.

Monsignor William E. F. Griffin, of St. Thomas Church, the Winona pro-cathedral, was the chairman Bishop Heffron appointed to organize all three events. He was also the master of ceremonies and one of the two cantors at the Terrace Heights ceremony.

The Winona Daily Republican-Herald praised the event. "The whole program of the day moved off smoothly and without a hitch anywhere, a large share of the credit for which was due to Reverend Father Griffin, who had general direction of all arrangements. Everything about the ceremonies at both buildings went off in a manner befitting the importance of the occasion.

"The walls of Saint Mary's College are now up to a level of the base of the second floor above the basement, and so the building's commanding location can be seen for a long distance. The building yesterday was covered with flags, with an immense flag waving from the top of the concrete distributing tower.

"The solemn ceremonies were opened with the chanting of the Litany of the Saints. After the robing of Bishop James Schwebach, of La Crosse, on the platform, Bishop Heffron, on behalf of Butler Brothers, contractors, presented to Bishop Schwebach a silver trowel, suitably engraved, with which to lay the cornerstone. In accepting the trowel, Bishop Schwebach expressed the hope that the building, the cornerstone of which was being laid, might endure for centuries and that prosperity might attend the educational work carried on therein. The locked box containing various articles was then placed in the cavity prepared for it in the large stone."

Bishop Heffron began his speech by describing the site. "Here nature has formed a natural terrace, and tableland that lends an entrancing view of the valley below with the Father of Waters beyond, and the beautiful city nestling toward the east, while the surrounding hills, with their rich verdure, bathed in sunlight, smile down upon the scene. Winona, taking her name from the most beautiful maiden of the tribe, according to familiar legend, is herself a beautiful city. In time to come and not far distant, another gem of beauty, like a crown of gold set

Engraving in a Minnesota atlas of the C. C. Beck property, 1872.

Bishop Joseph Cotter, shown in 1871, was a Liverpool native and 1850s immigrant. He was ordained in 1872 in St. Paul, Minnesota, as the first Bishop of Winona.

This 1911 map shows Winona's strategic location in the railroad network.

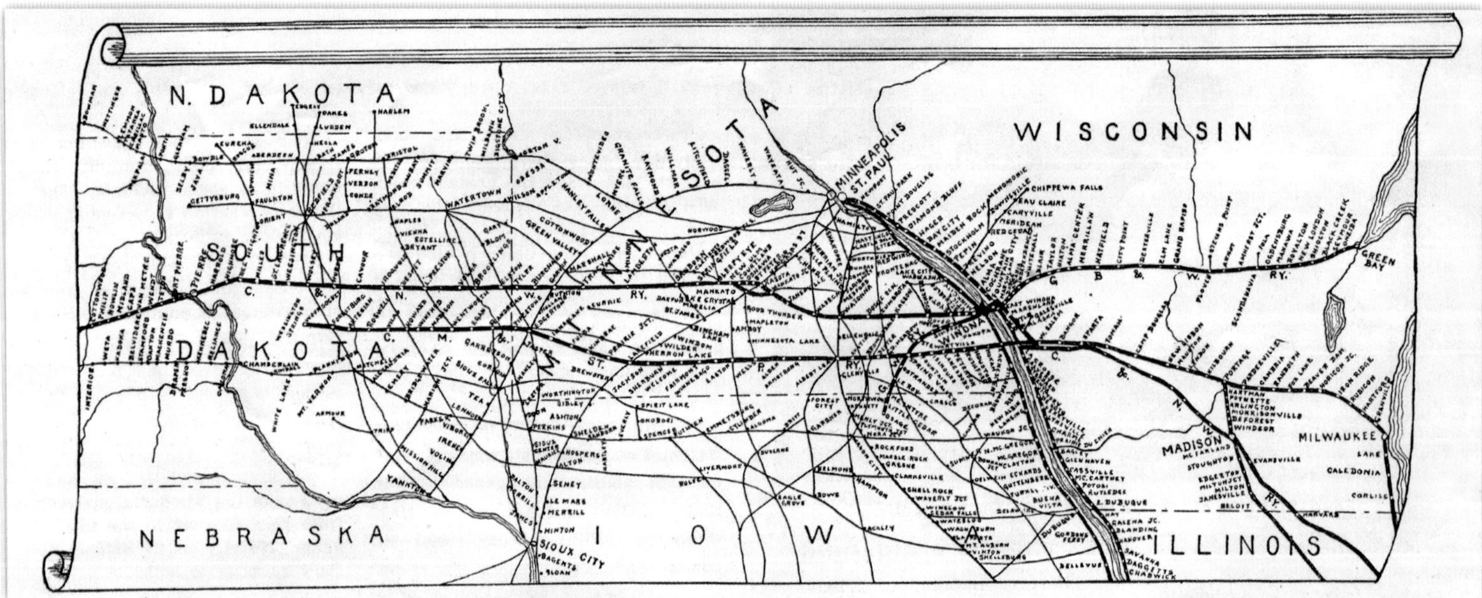

in an emerald background here on Terrace Heights will greet the admiring gaze of the thousands who shall pass to and fro. But it is not the material structure, massive and strong, nor the beauty of outline of a monumental edifice that will make the strongest appeal nor to which would we call present attention.

"St. Mary's College is established for the education and training of boys. It is intended to prepare the rising generation of young manhood, so far as they may avail themselves of its offices, for the duties of Christian manhood and citizenship of after life. The boy of today will be the man of tomorrow, and all the interests of society, the church and the state will be placed in his hands and confined to his keeping. How important it is, therefore, that he should be fitted for the work that awaits him.

"With this institution completed, the system will be practically rounded out. We already have primary and high schools for our boys and girls. We have the College of Saint Teresa for the higher education of women, and Saint Mary's College will be the final link in the chain of a complete system of primary and secondary education.

"Today we lay the cornerstone of this institution. At no distant day, under the smile of heaven and thanks to the generosity of our people, we shall gather again to dedicate a noble edifice to its God given work. And then the portals of St. Mary's will swing open to welcome the youth who shall flock hither in quest of culture, science and that training which can only be rightly imparted under the auspices of religious and Christian influence. And may the youth who pass through St. Mary's halls go forth to do valiant service for God, for country, for holy church and humanity."

In his remarks at the College of Saint Teresa, Bishop Heffron (the only speaker at both cornerstone ceremonies) praised the splendid educational work of the Sisters of Saint Francis. He concluded, "We have just come from the performance of a ceremony on Terrace Heights, which marks the inauguration of an institution destined to serve the purpose of higher education for boys. We have now witnessed a similar ceremony which initiates a new advance in the higher education of women. I want to say that a mighty achievement such as the Catholic educational system of the country does not exist as the work of the bishop and priest alone, but that it exists and thrives because the people believe in it, because the great heart of the people beats Godward. The people stand back of it. It is done with great sacrifice, but it is done with all the strength of living faith and love."

One hundred years later, the "tableland that lends an entrancing view of the valley below" remains a splendid location for a residential college. The trees that so vigorously and abundantly have grown in front of Saint Mary's Hall and Heffron Hall and on the slope that gave Terrace Heights its name provide beauty and shade but partially screen the entrancing view. For that view, Saint Mary's students and staff climb the bluffs, Baldy to the east (no longer bald) and Julius Point to the south (surrounded by tall trees).

A logo promoting Winona as a transportation center. In 1911, the passenger trains of five railroads served the city: Chicago, Burlington & Quincy (four trains daily in each direction), Chicago & Northwestern (three trains), Chicago Great Western (one train to Rochester), Chicago, Milwaukee & St. Paul (five trains), and Green Bay & Western (two trains).

Back to the Bishop's Challenge

In October 1910, six months after his installation as the second Bishop of Winona, Bishop Patrick R. Heffron inaugurated and sent to every Catholic family the diocesan newspaper, *The Courier*. The first issue announced his intention to open a Catholic high school for boys in Winona and to name it in honor of his predecessor, Bishop Cotter. He also published the "Proposed Plan for a College for Boys to be located somewhere in Southern Minnesota," including a two-page drawing of it. Many people assumed that Winona, the largest city in the diocese, was the obvious choice, but some business and civic leaders in Mankato, Lake City, Rochester, and Owatonna expressed interest in having the new college located in their community.

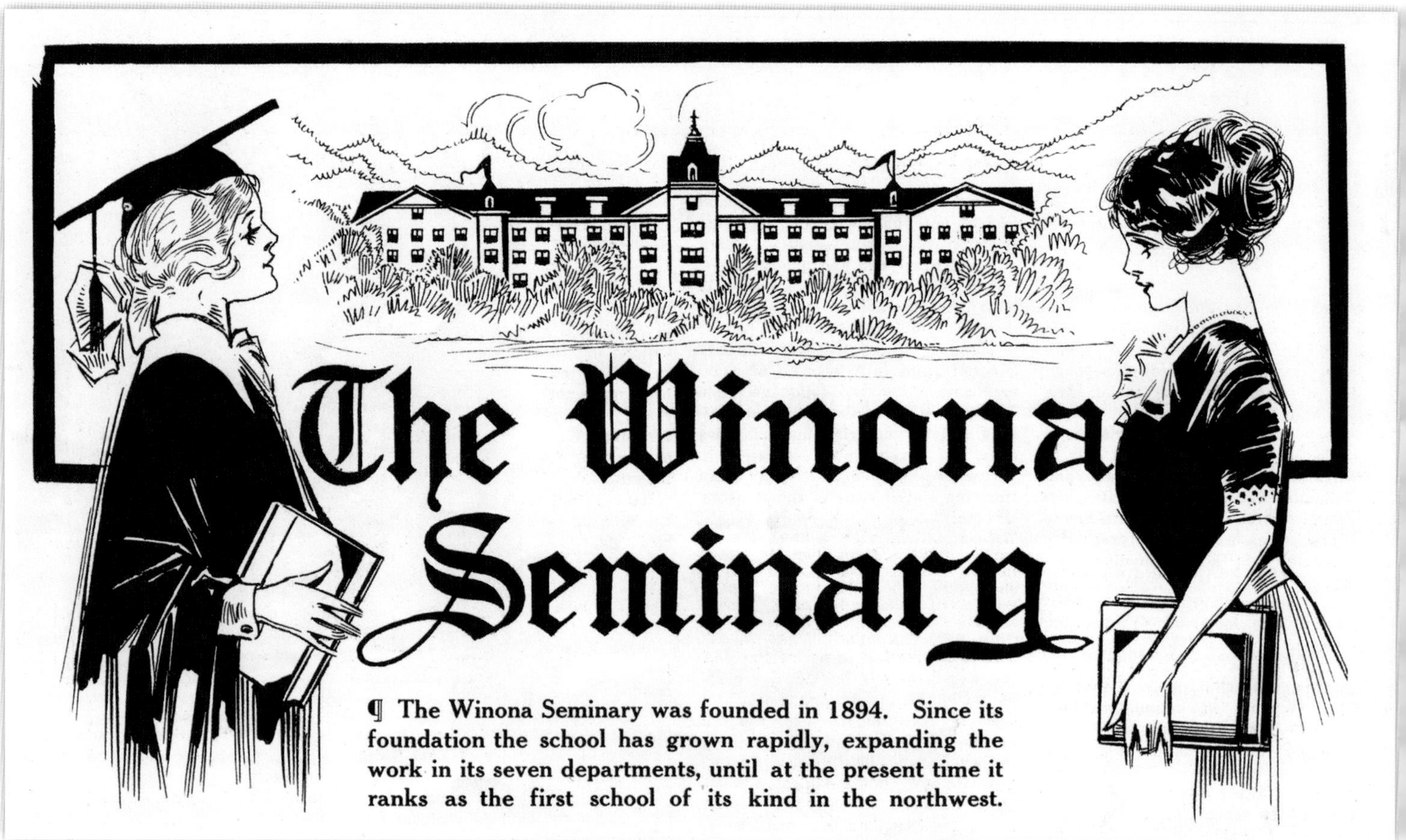

A 1900 newspaper advertisement for The Winona Seminary (College of Saint Teresa), founded in 1894 by Franciscan Sisters from Rochester.

Bishop Heffron let it be known that where he located the college would also be where he lived and administered the diocese. "It is entirely likely that the bishop will spend much of his time at the college and will reside either at the college or in the immediate vicinity," wrote Bishop Heffron in *The Courier*. "The home city of the bishop is not altogether a personal matter with him. Episcopal sees are sometimes changed when there are weighty reasons, but it is not at all a usual thing."

The threat that not locating the college in Winona might also cause the bishop to move galvanized Winona's civic leaders to secure the college for their city. Bishop Heffron wanted his new college for boys to compete with Saint John's College in Collegeville and the College of St. Thomas in St. Paul, but he realized that his college's location in a rural setting would attract students from a farm background.

Winona offered a location the city fathers thought perfect for the new school. The old C. C. Beck residence and 160-acre farm on Terrace Heights, above the West End, had already caught the bishop's eye. "The site is all that could be desired," he wrote in *The Courier*. "From the spot where the buildings would stand, the elevation affords a view of the city of Winona, the spires and domes of its buildings shooting up above the foliage of the trees; and further on is seen the lake, nestling along the foothills in the south, and still further, the valley that stretches down toward La Crosse." Bishop Heffron also noted "a charming vista between the hills, and through this vale courses a purling stream, rich with trout, and forming a dividing line between the mountain and the plain below."

The Winona Board of Trade appointed S. L. Prentiss to head a committee to secure the property for the new college. In January 1911, he notified the Board of Trade and Bishop Heffron that he had a $29,000 option on the 160 acres. He accepted the offer, and the Board of Trade transferred the property to the diocese before the bishop left in February 1911 for his first *ad limina* visit to Rome.

Winona was a bustling place in 1911. Back in 1870, it was the fourth largest wheat shipping port in the United States and a hugely successful sawmill center that processed millions of board feet of white pine timber. Besides being a manufacturing and a railroad hub, Winona was the county seat and a retail center for thousands of farmers in southern Minnesota and western Wisconsin. The completion of the Winona Railway Bridge across the Mississippi River in 1891 opened up rail traffic east into Wisconsin and south to Chicago. The population between 1900 and 1930 remained around 20,000.

Rt. Reverend Patrick Richard Heffron, shown in his 1910 passport photo, became the second Bishop of Winona on May 24, 1910, and served until his death on November 23, 1927.

NONA--THE CATHOLIC CENTER OF SOUTHERN MINNESOTA

›n the Diocese of Winona was d in the year 1889, the city of ıa was chosen as the seat of the diocese and has since enjoyed distinction. The bishop main- his residence in the city and the ıistration of this large diocese, ı composes the two lower tiers ›unties in southern Minnesota, Wabasha county, is done in the of Winona.

e Catholic population of the dio- numbers 60,000 souls, and one of that number reside in Wino- There are 120 parish churches

RT. REV. PATRICK R. HEFFRON,
Bishop of the Diocese of Winona.

and missions and 86 priests who attend them.

In Winona at the present time are five well defined parishes with flourishing schools attached. This number will soon be enlarged to six as at the present time St. Mary's chapel is being erected in the West End of the city and will be completed within a month or six weeks.

The following are the churches and their pastors:

Diocese of Winona—Rt. Rev. P. R. Heffron, Bishop; Rev. F. T. English, Secretary.

St. Thomas Pro-Cathedral—Rev. P. J. Gallagher, pastor; Rev. J. A. Parkinson, acting assistant.

St. Joseph's Church—Rev. J. Meier, pastor; Rev. P. A. Tibesar, assistant.

St. John's Church—Rev. F. T. English, pastor.

St. Stanislaus Church—Rev. J. Pacholski, pastor; Rev. J. Herek, assistant.

St. Casimir's Church—Rev. J. Grabowski, pastor.

Rt. Rev. J. B. Cotter, D. D., the first bishop of Winona, was, previous to his appointment as bishop, pastor of the St. Thomas parish for a number of years. Upon his death in June, 1909, Rt. Rev. P. R. Heffron was made second bishop of the diocese. He received official notification of his election to episcopate on the 4th day of March, 1910, and on May 19 took place the solemn service of consecration in the St. Mary's chapel of the St. Paul Seminary. On May 24, the city of Winona turned out en masse and cordially greeted the newly-consecrated bishop. Events of May 23 and 24 prove conclusively that Bishop Heffron has won a place in the hearts of all Winonans by virtue of his rank as bishop of the diocese of Winona and by reason of his eminence as an ecclesiastic and an educator and a leader.

The many words and hearty sentiments of welcome given him by Winonans generally marks the esteem in which Bishop Heffron is held by his fellow citizens.

Sketch of Bishop Heffron.

Following is a brief sketch of his life:

The Rt. Rev. Patrick Richard Heffron, the second bishop of Winona, was born in New York city, in 1860. When a child of six years he removed with his parents to Rochester, Minn., where the family has since resided. His primary education was secured in the schools of Mantorville and of Rochester. Later he entered St. John's College, Collegeville, Minn., for his classical course, and then proceeded to the Grand Seminary, Montreal, Canada, where after reading a distinguished course of six years in philosophy and theology, he was ordained by Archbishop Fabre of that city in the seminary chapel, December 22, 1884.

Returning to St. Paul he acted as assistant at the cathedral until 1885. In September of that year he was appointed professor at the newly founded St. Thomas' Seminary located in the city of St. Paul. There he remained until June, 1887. Then after a short pastorate at Osseo and at Albert Lea he went to Europe in October of the same year to pursue postgraduate work in theology. Most of his time abroad was devoted to study in Rome, but he also spent some time at the schools of Paris, Louvain, Innsburck and Oxford.

In May, 1889, he returned to St. Paul and was again appointed assistant at the cathedral as well as secretary to Archbishop Ireland. In this connection it may be said that the new bishop of Winona has been acting secretary of the archdiocese of St. Paul for the past twenty years.

In 1890 the future bishop was assigned to the cathedral as pastor, and remained in that capacity until 1896, when he was appointed professor at the new St. Paul seminary with the office of vice-rector. The ensuing year he was elevated to the rectorship of that institution, which office he held up to the time of his consecration as bishop of the diocese of Winona.

Rt. Rev. Bishop Heffron immediately outlined his work and began at once to put his plans into operation. Altho he has been bishop for only a little over one year, he already has a Boy's College well under way, which will cost in the neighborhood of $300,000.00 when completed. In appreciation of the bishop's labors in an educational direction and his willingness to locate this college in Winona, the citizens, when called upon by the Board of Trade, quickly raised the sum of $25,000.00 and purchased for him the Beck farm just to the west of the city, as a site for this large magnificent school which will serve as an educational center for the Catholic boys of southern Minnesota. This is, without question, one of the most beautiful sites for a college that could be found.

Another problem the bishop has worked out in the past year is a Boy's High school, which will bear the name of the late Bishop Cotter, "The Cotter High School." This is an undertaking on the part of the Catholics of the city of Winona and will cost close to $50,000.00 before completed. Bids have already been let for the erection of this building which will be located at the corner of Lafayette and Wabasha streets, the site having been purchased recently for this school. It is within one block of the cathedral property and an ideal location for a school of its kind. The Christian Brothers will be in charge of this institution and they will take up their residence in Winona within two or three weeks.

In looking to the future of Winona, Bishop Heffron realized that the city would build westward and saw the need of a parish in the extreme west end for his people. He is therefore having St. Mary's chapel erected just west of Vila street on the south side of Broadway, which will be the sixth Catholic church in Winona, and as the population increases in that part of the city, this undoubtedly will be known as St. Mary's parish.

The Catholic people of the city and diocese of Winona are furnished with a monthly paper known as The Winona Courier which is edited and published by Bishop Heffron as his official organ, and altho only eight numbers have been issued The Courier already enjoys a large circulation which is growing rapidly each month and it is only a question of time when every Catholic family in the diocese will be enrolled among the subscribers.

If the support that the city of Winona and the diocese of Winona has given the present bishop is continued the city will be acknowledged as one of the best Catholic educational centers of the northwest.

REV. FRANCIS T. ENGLISH,
Secretary to the Bishop and the Diocese.

Rev. F. T. English, secretary to the bishop, was born and raised in Winona, received his education at the St. Paul's seminary, St. Paul, and was ordained nine years ago. Previous to filling the position as secretary for the past five years, he was assistant pastor at the St. Thomas pro-Cathedral. He is recognized among the clergy throughout the state as being one of the most able priests of the diocese.

—16—

"Winona: The Catholic Center of Southern Minnesota" with photos of Bishop Patrick R. Heffron and Reverend Francis T. English.

Father Patrick R. Heffron, rector of the St. Paul Seminary, 1898–1910.

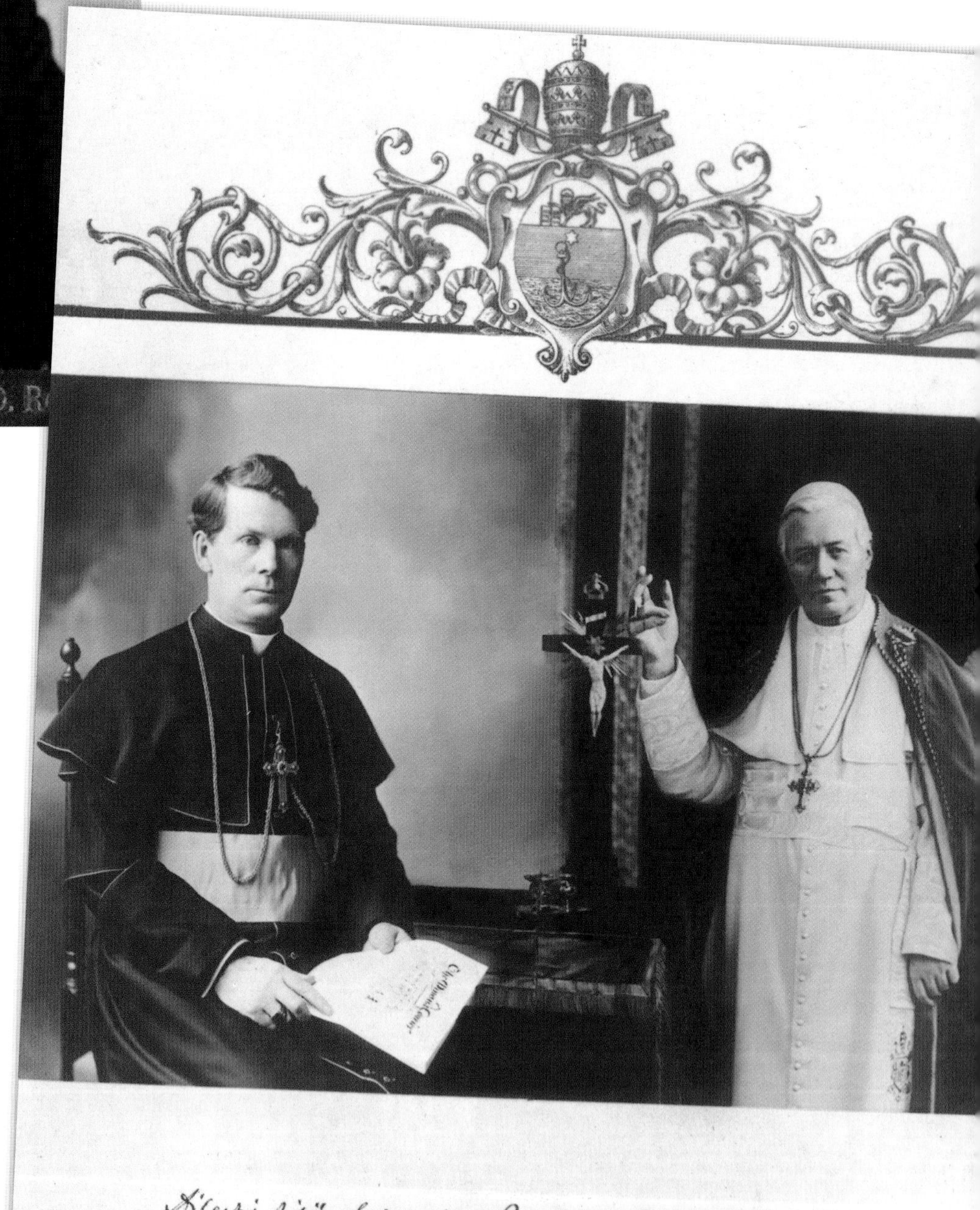

Bishop Patrick R. Heffron and Pope Pius X, March 8, 1911.

By Bishop Heffron's time, Winona was already a center of higher education. The Winona Normal School, founded in 1858 during the first session of the Minnesota State Legislature, was the first teacher training school built west of the Mississippi River. The Winona Seminary for Young Ladies had existed since 1894 and was flourishing under its new name, the College of Saint Teresa, later fondly known as "the Sem" by Saint Mary's students.

The Catholic population in Minnesota lived within the Diocese of St. Paul established in 1850 to include Minnesota, western Wisconsin, and the Dakotas. In 1889, Pope Leo XIII made St. Paul a province, with John Ireland its first archbishop, and created three new dioceses in Minnesota: Winona, St. Cloud, and Duluth. Father Joseph Bernard Cotter, a Winona priest, became the first Bishop of Winona, a diocese of some 30,000 Catholics living in the two southernmost tiers of Minnesota counties.

On his first *ad limina* visit to Rome since his installation in Winona on May 24, 1910, Bishop Heffron met with Pope Pius X on March 8, 1911. He reported his success in obtaining land for the new college, and he requested the Holy Father's blessing for the new venture. The Pope responded, "We earnestly pray that the Lord may be with our beloved sons, the faculty, professors, and students of the college established by our esteemed brother, the Bishop of Winona. We lovingly give them our apostolic blessing."

On his return trip from Rome, Bishop Heffron stopped in Belgium to visit the headquarters of the Brothers of the Christian Schools (Fratres Scholarum Christianarum). Already in 1910, he had written three times, without success, to Brother Emery Ildefonsus Curran, the provincial in St. Louis, requesting Brothers for the opening of Cotter High School for boys in Winona. Now Bishop Heffron appealed directly to the superior general, who endorsed his request and sent word to Brother Emery, who later traveled to Winona to arrange with Bishop Heffron for the Brothers to open classes at Cotter High School on September 5, 1911, in the St. Thomas Pro-Cathedral parish school. On December 3, 1911, Bishop Heffron dedicated the new Cotter High School building. He knew the Brothers during his years in St. Paul, where the cathedral pastor and future archbishop, Father John Ireland, after repeatedly being turned down, obtained Brothers for the cathedral school in November 1871 (only because the October 1871 Chicago Fire suddenly made Brothers available).

Rt. Reverend Patrick Richard Heffron

Rt. Reverend Patrick Richard Heffron was named Bishop of Winona on March 4, 1910, consecrated in the Saint Mary's Chapel of the St. Paul Seminary on May 19, 1910, and installed by Archbishop John Ireland in the St. Thomas Pro-Cathedral in Winona on May 24, 1910.

Patrick R. Heffron was born in New York City on June 1, 1859, of parents born in Ireland. When he was six years old, the family moved to Rochester, Minnesota. His primary education was in Mantorville and Rochester schools. After graduating from Saint John's College, Collegeville, Minnesota, he went to Montreal to attend the Grand Seminary, founded in 1840 by the Sulpicians. After six years of philosophy and theology, he was ordained to the priesthood on December 22, 1884, in the seminary chapel.

Father Heffron returned to St. Paul and assisted at the cathedral until September 1885, when he was appointed professor at the recently established St. Thomas Seminary in St. Paul. He remained there until June 1887. After a brief time at Osseo and at Albert Lea, he moved to Europe in October 1887 to do post-graduate work in theology. Most of his time abroad was in Rome, but he did visit schools in Paris, Louvain, Innsbruck, and Oxford.

In May 1889, Father Heffron returned to St. Paul and was again an assistant at the cathedral but received a new job as Archbishop Ireland's secretary. From 1890 to 1896, he was pastor of the cathedral and then was appointed professor and vice-rector at the new St. Paul seminary. One year later, he became rector, the office he held until his consecration as Bishop of the Diocese of Winona.

The front page of the first issue of the Winona Diocese's The Courier.

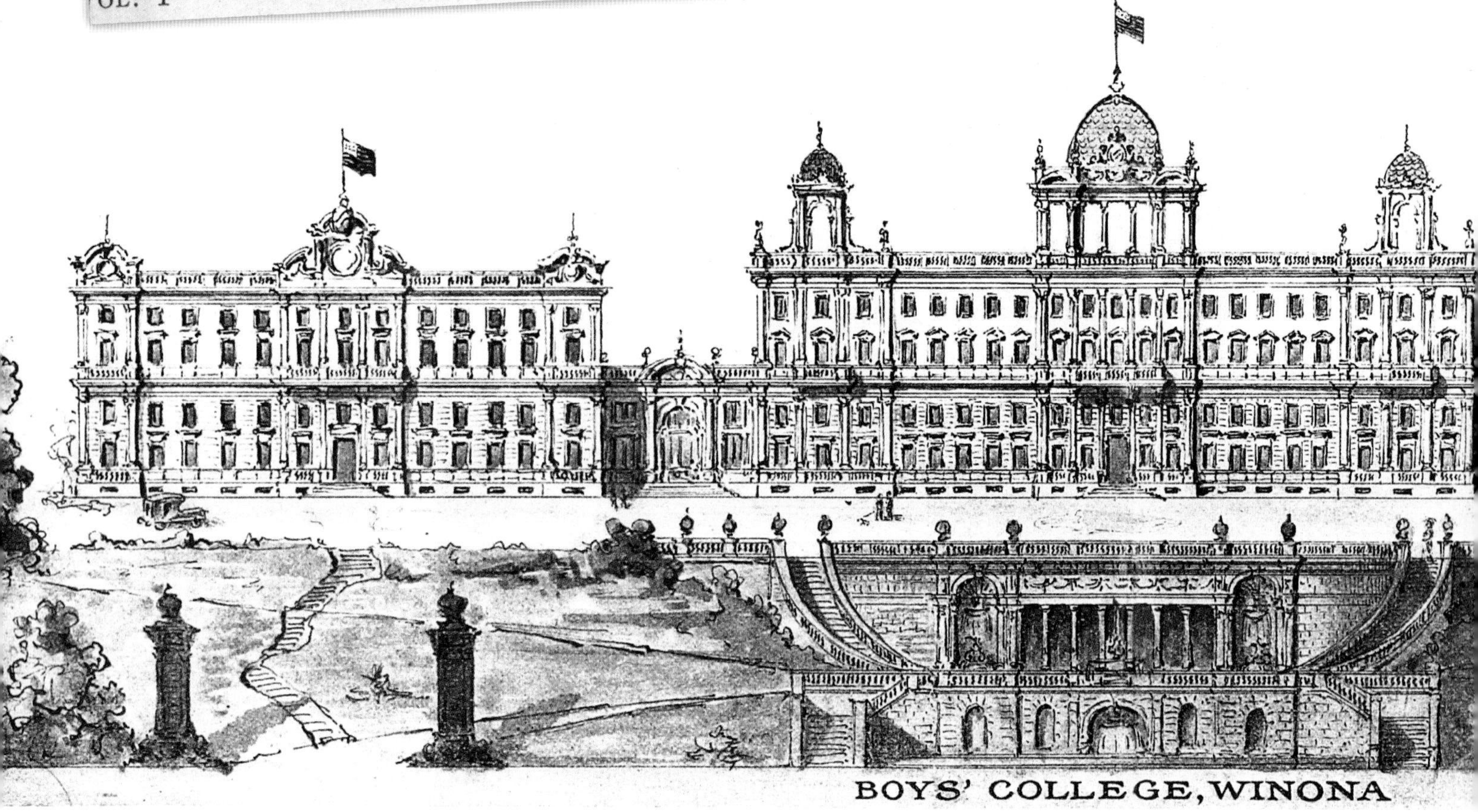

Aristide Leonori's design for Saint Mary's College, with the initial building at the right. The caption beneath this 1912 drawing states, "The building plans have been changed somewhat from this sketch."

Aristide Leonori, Roman architect of the first building of Saint Mary's College.

Building a Faculty and a Campus

Bishop Heffron knew that acquiring an excellent faculty for the new college would be one of his most important tasks, and he had a keen eye for talent. While in Rome in March 1911, he met with Julius W. Haun and three other Winona seminarians at the North American College. He encouraged Haun to continue his studies in English literature, which Haun would teach (especially Shakespeare and Milton, and then, by extension, Ethics) at Saint Mary's College for the next half-century.

Bishop Heffron contacted a prominent Roman architect with strong ties to the Vatican to design his new college. Aristide Leonori was designing the Santa Croce Church in Rome and the Coptic Christian Cathedral in Cairo. Well known by the U.S. hierarchy for his work on churches in St. Louis, Buffalo, and Washington, D.C., Leonori submitted a design for Saint Mary's College. As things turned out, other architects contributed to the design of Saint Mary's College (the building known as Saint Mary's Hall in later years).

The 1914 Saint Mary's College baseball team.

A sign of the times. Saint Mary's students stand by an early entrance sign.

Opening Day

Saint Mary's College opened on September 27, 1913, with about 100 students enrolled. One of the first teachers, Father Francis M. Kelly, who later succeeded Bishop Heffron as Bishop of Winona, prevailed upon his brother and sister-in-law in Houston, Minnesota, to send their son, Walt, to Saint Mary's. Young Kelly believed himself to be the first student to enroll there. Herman "Hub" Haberman, also in the original group, recalled years later that construction was still ongoing and that students had to walk across a wooden plank to get into the new building.

The college advertised across the diocese for students, touting the new building and dormitories that awaited students. "The College buildings are admirably fitted for their purpose," an advertisement in *The Courier* noted. "The buildings are of the latest fire-proof construction, large, roomy, ventilated in every room, heated and lighted throughout after the best modern systems. A fountain on each floor supplies fresh drinking water from an artesian well. The classrooms are bright and airy, and the living rooms afford every convenience for health and comfort. The infirmary is a cheerful and pleasant room. The dormitories, five in number, are arranged with the comfort and convenience of the student always in mind."

Bishop Heffron assembled an outstanding faculty for his new college, most of them priests from the diocese. Father William E. Griffin, the first rector, taught Latin, English, and Religion. Father John H. Peschges, the vice-rector, taught Christian Doctrine, Latin, and German. Father Herman J. McKenna, dean of discipline, taught Christian Doctrine and English. Father P. F. O'Connor taught the commercial subjects. Father Francis M. Kelly, D.D., taught Latin, Greek, and Mathematics.

One of the most accomplished scholars on the initial faculty was Father Patrick F. O'Brien, lured away

The graduating Class of 1919.

College transportation in 1916–17.

The Saint Mary's College Glee Club in 1918.

by Bishop Heffron from the College of St. Thomas. He earned an M.A. from Trinity College in Dublin and anchored the liberal arts curriculum of Saint Mary's College, teaching Latin, English, and History. He earned an excellent reputation for the college in the classics, and he wrote and lectured extensively and regularly wrote a column in *The Courier* on a wide range of topics.

Julius W. Haun, a native of Winona, returned from his studies in Rome, was ordained in Winona on October 28, 1915, and immediately began teaching at Saint Mary's College. He had studied at Winona Normal School and the College of St. Thomas, St. Paul, and while living at the North American College in Rome, he earned doctoral degrees in philosophy and in theology from the Urban University of Rome. From 1918 to 1933, he served as dean at Saint Mary's College, where he remained a professor until 1956. Saint Mary's College honored him with the degree of Doctor of Education, *honoris causa*, in 1956. That same year, he became the pastor of St. Casimir parish in Winona, which he served until his retirement in 1968. He was active in the Catholic Education Association and served as president of the College Section and as a member of the Executive Committee. Pope Pius XII named him a domestic prelate on October 13, 1943, and Pope John XXIII bestowed on him the papal honor and title of Prothonotary Apostolic on May 26, 1962.

Father Nicholas Corona joined the faculty in 1917 after being expelled from his native Mexico during the Mexican Revolution. He later returned to Mexico as a bishop. Father Thomas Normoyle, a classics professor, was mourned by the entire student body and faculty when he died during the influenza pandemic of October 1918. Father Ambrose L. McGreevey taught a number of subjects and coached several sports teams.

During its first decade, Saint Mary's College was both a secondary school and a college, initially including an agriculture curriculum so that students could learn scientific agriculture. In the early decades of the 20th century, obtaining a diploma from a four-year academic high school (some were called academies) became a priority. Then college attendance became increasingly desirable and possible; Saint Mary's College was able to provide both levels of higher education.

Athletics was a part of student life from the outset. In October 1913, the student body voted to organize an athletic association under Coach McGreevey and fielded football, basketball, and baseball teams. In 1914, the administration created an intramural program and encouraged all students to participate. The first intramural sport was basketball.

The faculty organized informal debates and created a library on the third floor in the winter of 1914. Many books were donations from the faculty, and the library provided students a growing collection of magazines and hometown southern Minnesota newspapers. Students presented their first play, *The College Freshman*, just before Christmas in 1913. Extracurricular activities began to appear during the college's first four years. By 1917, students could join a number of campus clubs and societies, including the League of the Sacred Heart, Sodality of the Blessed Virgin, Debating Society, Sanctuary Society, College Choir, College Glee Club, and Commercial Club.

Saint Mary's College, a 1919 panoramic view from the bluff to the west. The distant bluffs, Baldy (left) and Julius Point, are not yet completely forested.

In the early years, enrollment remained relatively stable. There were 105 students in the 1913–14 academic year, and an average of nearly 125 students each year through the spring of 1917. While Saint Mary's continued to strengthen the faculty and to add college-level courses, the junior high school program ended in 1919, and the high school program began phasing out in 1925.

An Assassination Attempt

Perhaps the strangest event in the college's history occurred in August 1915, just weeks before the third year of operation began. Bishop Heffron, then 56, was saying morning Mass in his private chapel at the college when a diocesan priest, Father Laurence Lesches, rushed in and fired four pistol shots at the bishop. Two found their mark, one in the chest, perilously close to a lung. Local doctors, assisted by Dr. Will Mayo, who had rushed to Winona from Rochester when he heard the news, oversaw triage until they could safely move the bishop to Saint Mary's Hospital in Rochester under Dr. Mayo's care.

Bishop Heffron, who spent much of the next two months recuperating, directed that the diocese pay for the defense of Father Lesches during the trial held that winter. He had known the priest for nearly 20 years, since the late 1890s, when Father Lesches was enrolled at the St. Paul Seminary.

The case scandalized Winona and southern Minnesota and was covered extensively in local newspapers. At his trial in December 1915, Lesches was judged innocent by reason of insanity and committed to

Saint Peter State Hospital, where he resided until his death on January 10, 1943.

Bishop Heffron recovered from the attack and returned to the affairs of his diocese and his college. For Saint Mary's, the three years following the 1915 attack were a time of challenge and opportunity, including World War I and the influenza pandemic that descended upon Minnesota in the fall of 1918.

War and Peace

The formal declaration of war against the Imperial German Government, on April 6, 1917, brought the United States into the world conflict already raging for nearly three years. The World War I era was difficult for Saint Mary's College. Around 53 students and alumni served in the military, and one alumnus was killed in action during the war. Enrollment dropped from 125 students to 107 during the 1917–18 academic year, recovered to 140 in 1918–19, and increased more than 40 percent to 202 students in 1919–20.

The Student Army Training Corps (SATC), a nationwide program of the War Department during World War I, began in the spring of 1918 and ended in December that year. Saint Mary's College was one of 157 schools accepted for the program in the 1918–19 academic year. Saint Mary's students donned uniforms and drilled to the commands of an SATC officer. At first, excitement about the Corps appealed to students, but after the Armistice of November 11, 1918, the novelty quickly wore off. The U.S. government disbanded the SATC in the spring of 1919.

The Saint Mary's College dairy farm, begun in 1914, provided ample work for students taking courses such as Botany, Farm Crops, Grain Crops, Grains and Fertilizers, Dairying and Livestock, Horticulture, and Farm Management. In 1918, the college phased out the agricultural program but kept the farm.

Financing Growth

To finance scholarships, professorships, department chairs, and salaries, Bishop Heffron in 1912 established an endowment fund from contributions by people in the diocese, which *The Courier* periodically highlighted by publishing the names of contributors.

The endowment fund was sufficient to finance growth during the first seven years of operation, but by 1920 enrollment was growing well beyond the average of the early years. Because Saint Mary's College needed a major new source of capital, Bishop Heffron and his advisors announced a major capital campaign in 1919 to finance the new buildings and departments that Saint Mary's College needed to move from a combination high school and junior college to an accredited four-year liberal arts college.

Pledges poured in during 1919 and 1920, and Saint Mary's College began construction in the spring of 1920 of the new residence hall (named Heffron Hall after the bishop's death in 1927) and attached bi-level gymnasium (later named Skemp Hall) to meet the anticipated peacetime wave of new students from Minnesota, Wisconsin, and the Dakotas. Bishop Heffron chose architect Clarence H. Johnston of St. Paul to design the residence hall.

Because of the farm recession of the late 1920s and early 1930s, many of the 1919 and 1920 pledges remained unpaid, a situation that led to considerable financial problems for Saint Mary's College during the Great Depression.

Of the 11 faculty members, all priests, who were living on campus in 1920, according to the federal census of January 26, 1920, seven were born in Minnesota: Father John H. Peschges, the rector and future Bishop of Crookston; Father Herman A. Baecker; Father Peter W. Bartholome, future Bishop of St. Cloud; Father William F. Coleman; Father Julius W. Haun; Father Frank M. Kelly, future Bishop of Winona; and Father Frank A. McMahon. Two were born in Iowa, Father Ambrose L. McGreevey and Father John H. Stager. Two others were immigrants with naturalization papers, Father Charles A. Cavanagh, born in England, and Father Patrick F. O'Brien, born in Ireland. Not counting Father Peschges, Father Cavanagh, and Father O'Brien, the average age of the other eight teachers was just below 30.

The 1920 census also lists among the campus residents eight Sisters and eight other single women, all working as domestics; three men described as janitors; one fireman; and one office boy, all working either at the college or at the bishop's residence.

Monsignor William E. Francis Griffin
1st President, 1912–1918

Monsignor William E. Francis Griffin, born in Rochester, New York, in 1875 of parents born in Ireland, became a priest of the Winona Diocese after studying at the St. Paul Seminary, where the future bishop, Patrick R. Heffron, was rector. Monsignor Griffin served as Bishop Heffron's on-site rector at Saint Mary's College for six years.

A seasoned organizer and an excellent singer, Monsignor Griffin led an equally talented and zealous team of priests and laymen who covered all aspects of the initial secondary school and junior college curriculum, including business and commerce, science and mathematics, theology, and the other liberal arts. Monsignor Griffin taught Latin, English, and Religion.

During his years as rector, Monsignor Griffin oversaw the organization of Saint Mary's College into three levels of study: academy (high school completion), junior college, and commercial. He encouraged the students to form athletic teams, and he helped them to schedule competitions with nearby high schools and colleges. He supervised the establishment of the Student Army Training Corps (SATC) at Saint Mary's during the 1917–18 academic year.

In the spring of 1918, Monsignor Griffin asked Bishop Heffron to assign him to a parish, his first love. He was a beloved monsignor in the Winona Diocese throughout his life. He returned to celebrate with Saint Mary's on the occasion of its 25th anniversary in 1938. He died in Rochester, Minnesota, in November 1946, and is buried in Austin, Minnesota.

Students in the Student Army Training Corps (SATC) in 1918.

Fifty-three student cadets and officers in front of Saint Mary's College in 1918. At an assembly in late 1918, Father John Peschges, the rector, expelled three students, and a student body strike ensued. He restored order by giving the students a free day. Bishop Heffron told the 140 students that the college must adhere to a contract with the Student Army Training Corps until the end of 1918.

In the 1920s, Saint Mary's added a pre-engineering course and introduced General College Mathematics, Technical Drawing, and Descriptive Geometry. The science and pre-medical curriculum added Physics and Organic Chemistry. The departments of Philosophy and Education, established in 1924, introduced the General Ethics course. By the middle of the decade, the library had grown to 5,100 books, many of them selected by Father Edward J. Lynch, the librarian.

The 1920 faculty included Dr. John J. Hoffman, in his first year at Saint Mary's, who founded the Chemistry Department and taught at the college until 1962. Like many of the early faculty members, he was broadly and deeply educated. In addition to Chemistry, he taught Mathematics, Biology, Physics, Education, Latin, and Modern Languages. A graduate of St. John's University, Collegeville, Minnesota, he did graduate work at the University of Minnesota and earned a Ph.D. in Chemistry at the University of Chicago. In 1960, Saint Mary's College awarded him the Doctor of Law degree, *honoris causa*. The Christian Brothers affiliated him to their Institute, and the Pope made him a Knight of St. Gregory.

Extracurricular activities expanded during the 1920s. In 1926, students formed a Dramatic Club and performed a trio of one-act plays. The Columbus Day Frolic became a tradition. *The Alumni Bulletin*, a newspaper for alumni and students, gave way to *The Nexus* in 1925.

Expanded academic offerings and the 1926 accreditation by the Catholic Education Association enabled Saint Mary's College to begin phasing out the high school department in 1927. The last high school class graduated in 1929, the year when the college was preparing for accreditation by the North Central Association as a four-year college.

Student Army Training Corps, 1919.

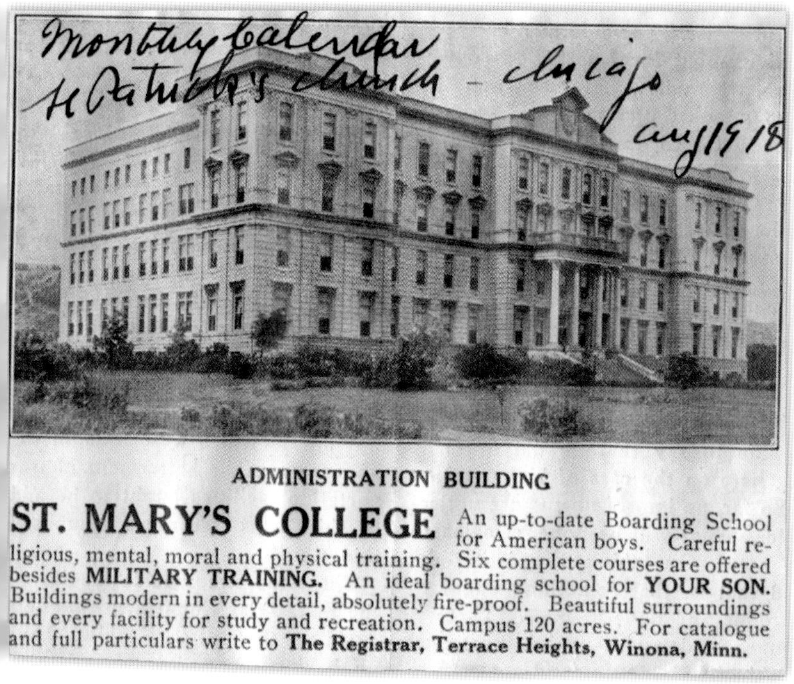

An advertisement in the August 1918 monthly calendar of St. Patrick Catholic Church, Chicago.

The 1918 Saint Mary's College football team.

Minnesota Intercollegiate Athletic Conference

From the beginning, Saint Mary's College valued and encouraged participation in intercollegiate athletics. Coach Thomas J. Skemp's arrival on campus in 1919 ushered in an era of football dominance. A hard taskmaster, he urged his players to "do your part and make yourself a good cog in a perfect machine." The football team went 5-1 in 1924 and compiled a 6-1 record in 1925. In 1926, Saint Mary's College joined the Minnesota Intercollegiate Athletic Conference (MIAC).

In 1927, its second year in the MIAC, Saint Mary's dominated football by going undefeated. The team scored 164 points during the season and allowed opponents only 18 points in the eight games played.

The success in football carried over into the hockey program, which began in the late 1920s. The team compiled a record of 11-2-1 in 1929–30, winning the MIAC championship over the College of St. Thomas. The 1930–31 hockey team played such eastern powerhouses as the University of Michigan, Princeton, and Yale and boasted two All-Americans on its roster, Tony Prelesnik and goalie Oscar Almquist.

The logo, nickname, and uniform colors of Saint Mary's College athletic teams have their own history. Between 1913 and 1926, the initial nicknames were "Maroon and White" and "Maroon Men," because of the original maroon and white colors of the team uniforms. When Saint Mary's College changed its school colors to cardinal red and white in 1926, people began describing the teams as "Cardinals." The nickname changed in 1932 to "Redmen," and the Native American image came into use. When Saint Mary's College began enrolling women in 1969, the women's varsity athletic teams received a separate nickname, "Cardinals," and the men's teams stayed with "Redmen."

An internal debate about the use of "Redmen" began on campus in the early 1970s. In the 1988–89 academic year, after receiving a request from a Minnesota Native American organization, Saint Mary's College became one of the first colleges in the country to change its name and logo as a result of this movement. The college assigned the Cardinals nickname to men's and women's athletic teams and adopted the Cardinal, now referred to as "Big Red," as logo and mascot.

The 1920 football team (above) and its coach, Tom Skemp (left). Saint Mary's College lost to the College of St. Thomas by one point in 1920, despite the Herculean efforts of fullback Dick Hudson, the college's first African-American athlete.

The 1919 fundraising dinner in the Saint Mary's College dining hall. Bishop Heffron introduced Father Francis M. Kelly, vice-rector, professor, and future Bishop of Winona, as the Million Dollar Building and Endowment Campaign leader.

The End of an Era

During its undefeated 1927 football season, Saint Mary's College suffered its greatest loss since its founding. On the Wednesday before Thanksgiving, Bishop Patrick R. Heffron died as a result of the facial cancer that he suffered during his last year on earth. Then 67, Bishop Heffron had long since left the college in the hands of Monsignor John Peschges, the rector, and Monsignor Francis M. Kelly, the vice-rector; both later became bishops. In 1928, Pius XI named Monsignor Kelly the third Bishop of Winona, and in 1938, he appointed Monsignor Peschges the second Bishop of Crookston, Minnesota.

The death of Bishop Heffron marked the end of an era for Saint Mary's College. He did not live to see the Great Depression, which devastated the finances of his beloved Saint Mary's. When he died on November 23, 1927, Saint Mary's College was an academic, athletic, and civic success, and some of the original faculty were still active.

The Winona Republican-Herald summed up Bishop Heffron's career, ending on a poignant note about his interest in athletics: "The development of higher Catholic education, which has placed the diocese of Winona in the lead in this field of endeavor, was the crowning achievement in the life of the Rt. Reverend Patrick R. Heffron, D.D., bishop of the diocese of Winona.

"Thirty-five Catholic high schools, most of which originated during his administration, the largest numerical representation of any diocese in the United States, including the large dioceses of Chicago and New York, stand today to perpetuate his memory.

The 1919 goal was $1 million in four months (equivalent to $13 million in 2012 dollars).

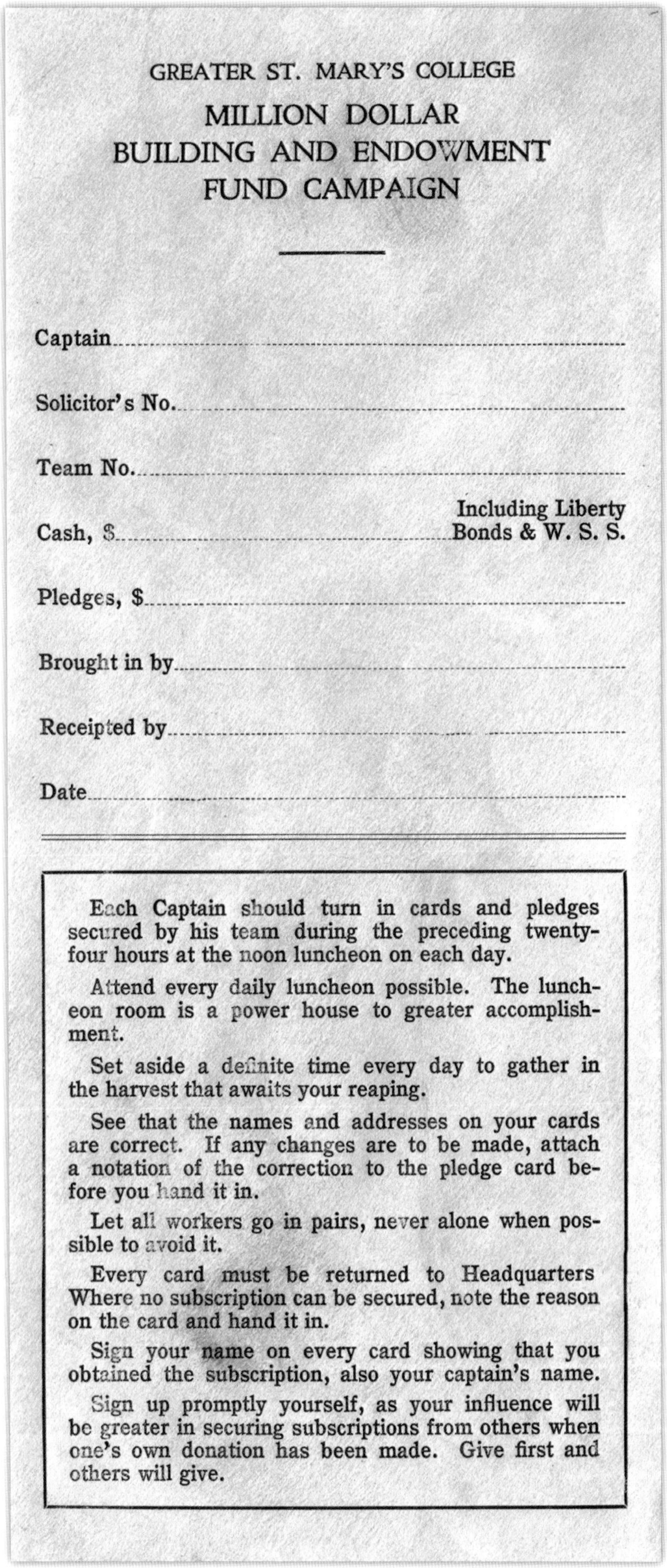

GREATER ST. MARY'S COLLEGE

MILLION DOLLAR
BUILDING AND ENDOWMENT
FUND CAMPAIGN

Captain..........

Solicitor's No..........

Team No..........

Cash, $.......... Including Liberty Bonds & W. S. S.

Pledges, $..........

Brought in by..........

Receipted by..........

Date..........

Each Captain should turn in cards and pledges secured by his team during the preceding twenty-four hours at the noon luncheon on each day.

Attend every daily luncheon possible. The luncheon room is a power house to greater accomplishment.

Set aside a definite time every day to gather in the harvest that awaits your reaping.

See that the names and addresses on your cards are correct. If any changes are to be made, attach a notation of the correction to the pledge card before you hand it in.

Let all workers go in pairs, never alone when possible to avoid it.

Every card must be returned to Headquarters Where no subscription can be secured, note the reason on the card and hand it in.

Sign your name on every card showing that you obtained the subscription, also your captain's name.

Sign up promptly yourself, as your influence will be greater in securing subscriptions from others when one's own donation has been made. Give first and others will give.

A pledge card for the 1919 Million Dollar Building and Endowment Campaign.

"At the time of his elevation to the episcopacy, few parishes had their own high schools. One year after assuming the new duties, he had erected in Winona the Cotter School for Boys in memory of the late Bishop Cotter. The materialization of this important project, one of the first of a long list of high schools to follow throughout the diocese, including Heffron High of Rochester, was realized in 1911. The school here affords Catholic young men an education under the direction of the Christian Brothers. St. Mary's College stands as the master achievement in the active life of Bishop Heffron. It will perpetuate his memory.

"He took special interest in the physical as well as the mental development of the young people in high school and college and encouraged athletic contests by his presence. Only recently he attended several football games in which St. Mary's and Cotter High were participants, watching the proceedings from an enclosed automobile. On Sunday he inquired about the outcome of the game between Cotter and La Crosse High."

The changing nature of the Saint Mary's College faculty after the death of Bishop Heffron is indicated by the 1930 federal census, April 28, 1930, which lists only three Catholic priests living on the Saint Mary's College campus who were also living there in 1920: Monsignor John H. Peschges, the president; Father Julius Haun; and Bishop Francis Kelly, now Bishop of Winona, who was living in the former C. C. Beck house. Bishop Kelly's housekeeper is also listed, Anna M. Cassidy.

Eight priests living at Saint Mary's College at the time of the 1920 census are not listed as residing there in 1930. One new resident Catholic priest at the college in 1930 was Father Webster Kenning, born in Illinois. Seven single men are listed as Saint Mary's College residents. Two are described as professors, Robert J. Woods, born in Massachusetts, and Laurence J. McHugh, born in Minnesota, and five are listed as teachers: Joseph B. Collins, John Gruber, John K. Ryan, and Frank Sullivan, all four born in Minnesota, and Edward Lynch, born in Canada. Nicholas J. Musty, born in Minnesota and recently married, is listed as the coach, but his wife's name is not included. One resident student is also on the list, Francis A. Pankert, single, born in Czechoslovakia.

Also included on the 1930 federal census as residents at Saint Mary's College are seven Sisters and four other single women who were in domestic service, plus a steam engineer and his wife and two children, and six single or widowed men: one janitor, one carpenter, two laborers, and two herdsmen. Four of the seven Sisters were also listed in 1920 at Saint Mary's College: Sisters M. DePaul, M. Teresa, M. Pelagia, and M. Regina.

The cover of the 1919 Saint Mary's College campaign book.

The power house, shown in 1923, was eventually named the Kulas-Connaughty Power House in honor of Max Kulas and Roger Connaughty, two long-time superintendents of maintenance at Saint Mary's College.

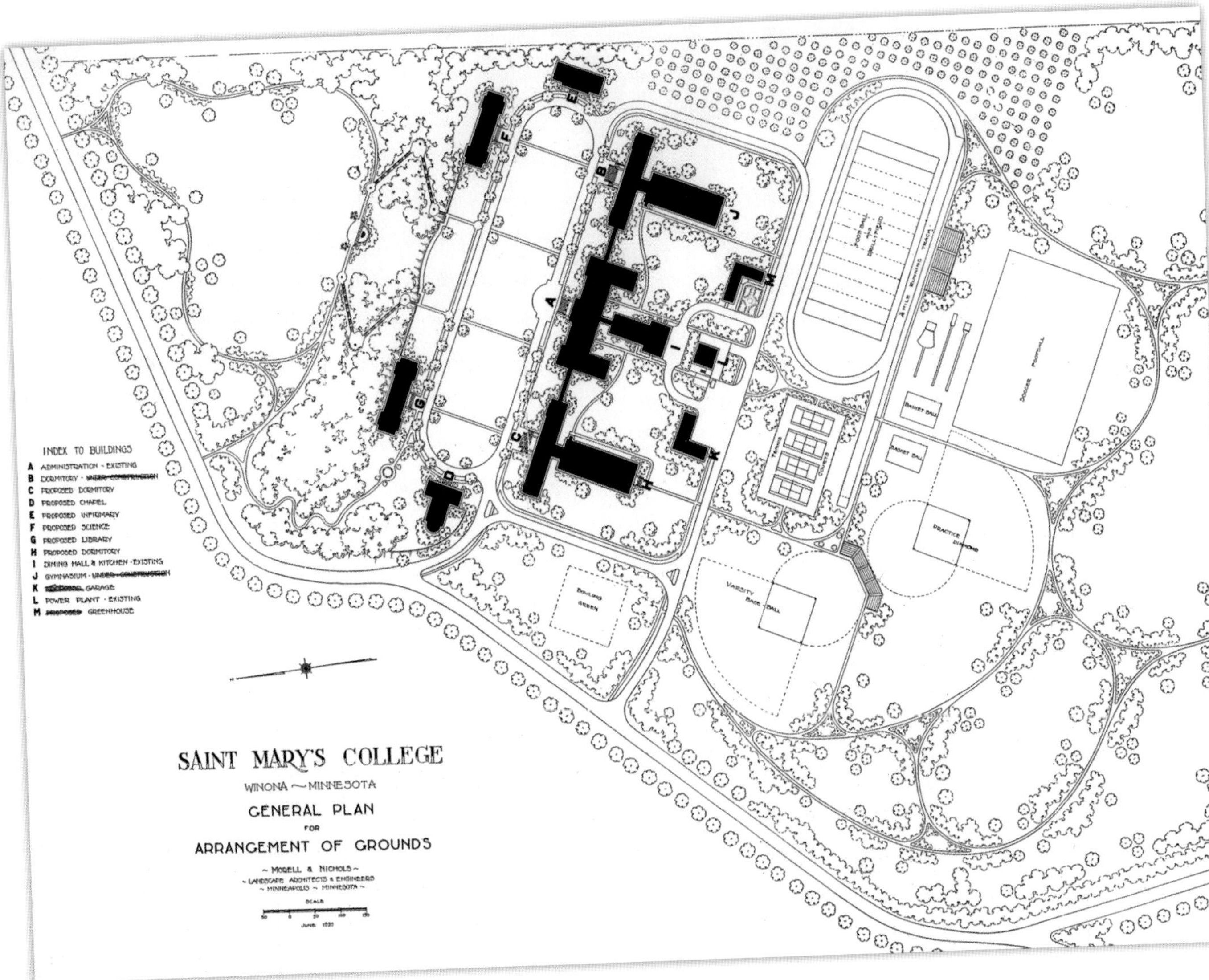

The 1920 campus plan, designed in anticipation of a postwar increase in enrollment.

The new student residence hall under construction in 1921. It was named in honor of Bishop Heffron after his death in 1927.

Monsignor John Hubert Peschges
2nd President, 1918–1933

Monsignor John Hubert Peschges, known on campus as "the friendly one," was born in Minnesota of parents born in Germany. Bishop Patrick R. Heffron appointed him in 1918 to be the second rector of Saint Mary's College. Like his predecessor, Monsignor Griffin, his elder by six years, Monsignor Peschges was a student at the St. Paul Seminary when Bishop Heffron was rector there. After his ordination, he was assistant pastor at the Catholic mission in Excelsior, Minnesota.

A Latin scholar, Monsignor Peschges also taught English, Greek, and German at Saint Mary's. He phased out the high school program but made sure that students already enrolled could graduate. He conducted the successful capital campaign for the construction of a new residence hall (Heffron Hall) and two-level gymnasium (Skemp Hall).

Monsignor Peschges expanded the curriculum, increased the enrollment, and established the tone of access and approachability that has characterized Saint Mary's throughout the years. In 1926, he awarded diplomas to the first class (10 students) to complete the four-year degree at Saint Mary's.

Monsignor Peschges became the second Bishop of the Crookston, Minnesota diocese on November 18, 1938. He was known there as a tolerant, broad-minded supporter of the small farmer, of civic projects, and of hunting and fishing.

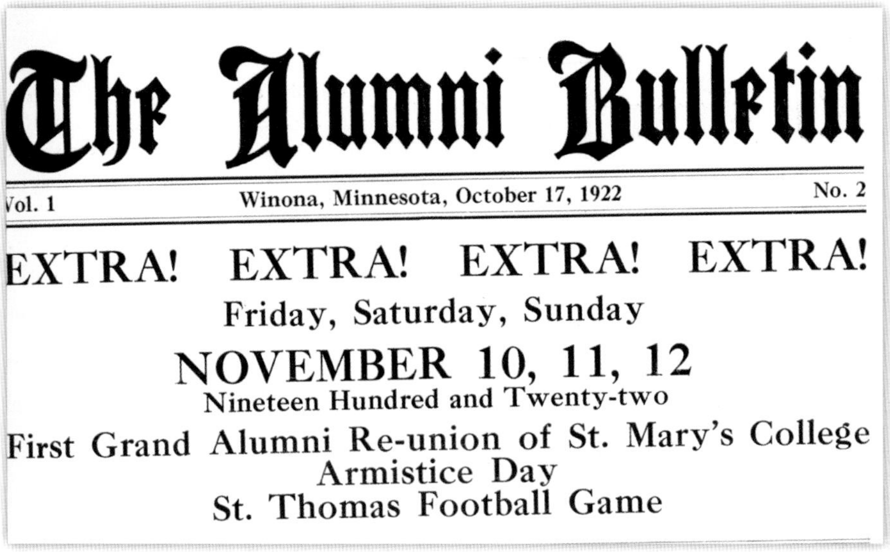

The Alumni Bulletin

Vol. 1 — Winona, Minnesota, October 17, 1922 — No. 2

EXTRA! EXTRA! EXTRA! EXTRA!

Friday, Saturday, Sunday

NOVEMBER 10, 11, 12

Nineteen Hundred and Twenty-two

First Grand Alumni Re-union of St. Mary's College

Armistice Day

St. Thomas Football Game

A homecoming alert in The Alumni Bulletin, *October 17, 1922. Saint Mary's College lost the 1922 game but defeated the Tommies in the homecoming game in 1923.*

A cartoon for the November 1923 football game between Saint Mary's College and the Fort Snelling team.

A 1920s view of Saint Mary's College, perhaps taken by a hiker climbing Baldy.

The five members of the Class of 1920 pictured with Father Patrick O'Brien.

The Alumni Bulletin

Vol. 1 | Winona, Minnesota, September 27, 1922 | No. 1

KEY-NOTE OF THE NEW CRUSADE

Memory's halls are crowded with the faces of yester-years—voices come echoing across the moors of time, and in the heart the fires of desire burn high again just for a day with old College pals. And with this bar, we have struck the chord in the heart of the Alumnus that calls loudest for effecting an organization among the former boys of the old Alma Mater.

No one ever understands us like our old College Pals, to them we have whispered our ambitions and listened in turn to the story of their hopes and fears. In the class-room and on the campus unions have formed every link golden friendship forged in the fires of a common sympathy, in work and at play.

Time too has made our reverent respect for Alma Mater still more sacrosanct, verily she is the avatar of our highest ideals. It was the birth-place of inspiration that has been to the Alumnus a guiding star; Alumni Day will sink deeper that inspiration in the soul, the forces of yesterday will be mobilized with those of today, ambitions have been realized, dreams have come true, and it will hearten us to hear the story first-hand; Fortune may have smiled and adversity too may have played its part but the Democracy of good-will never absent in such gatherings will quicken the spirit for greater effort and steel the heart in what might seem failure.

Neither the tyrrany of work nor the voice of common-place pleasantries will stay the march of a real man on his way to Alumni-Day, for ten thousand welcomes await him at the port where he lifted anchor.

COLLEGE ACTIVITIES

The college reopened on September the 4th with its usual number of old and new faces,—new faces—non-plussed by their new surroundings, downcast and heartsick at the thought of leaving home. Even the old students are effected in this manner to some extent. The faces of the majority, however, are beaming with delight at the meeting of their old friends and professors. "How are you, Bill?" "Fine. How are you?" "Did you have a good vacation?" "Glad to see you back." "It feels pretty good to get back," are the words ringing thru the college halls and over the campus. The increase in enrollment is substantial. The college section especially has a notable increase in its numbers. The daily routine of study and class has set in. At this writing, every one is settled for the year.

It may be interesting to know who constitutes the faculty at St. Mary's this year, since the relationship of faculty and student body has always been very close. Fr. Peschges is Rector. Fr. Haun, Dean of Studies. Fr. Coleman, Dean of Discipline. Fr. Galligan, Dean of New Hall. Fr. Muyssen, Fr. McGreevy, Fr. Woods, Fr. Bartholome are on the teaching staff. Mr. Hoffman, Mr. Skemp, Mr. Brungart, and Mr. Wagner, who was on the staff in 1912, constitute the lay faculty.

On August 22nd the college halls and campus were the scene of a magnificent event. The Heights were aroused from the sleepy slumbers of vacation to witness the dedication of the New Hall and gymnasium.

People and priests from the various parts of the diocese gathered in the gymnasium, where a temporary Altar had been erected. Bishop Heffron, in solemn procession with the clergy blessed the new buildings. Rt. Rev. Joseph G. Pinton, Bishop of Superior sang a Pontifical High Mass at which Dr. Robert Condon of LaCrosse preached an eloquent sermon. The musical talent of the choirs of Winona sang the mass.

After the dedication luncheon was served to all the visitors. The Rollingstone band rendered a concert. A baseball game, arranged by Lawrence McHugh, between the Alumni and Kellogg, the champions of Wabasha County, was played in the afternoon. Sorry to say, the Alumni were beaten 4 to 1.

The day as a whole was a success. It was estimated that over a thousand people were present. All went away, feeling that they had an institution in the diocese of Winona that they could be well proud of.

A new step taken by the Bishop at St. Mary's college, is the Retreat for Laymen. It began three days prior to the dedication of the new buildings. Fr. Mertz S. J. of Loyola U. Chicago, preached the retreat. The men, thirty-five in number—some of whom were Alumni—enjoyed it very much. The Alumni now have the opportunity to continue the yearly retreats which they made while at college.

The Science department under the direction of Mr. Hoffman and Mr. Wagner, has been generously brought up to the standards of the university requirements. New laboratory tables and chemical and biological equipment of all kinds are being placed in the new rooms set aside for that purpose. The air is to be filled with the dying croaks of murdered frogs and saturated with aromatic fumes of chemical changes.

The members of the Philharmonic society responded very enthusiastically to the call of Professor Brungart to reorganize the band, orchestra, choir and Glee Club. Professor Brungart, a talented musician from Kansas City, is beginning his work at St. Mary's College this year, succeeding Mr. Endres. The musical standards of former years will, no doubt, be

(Continued on Page 2)

The Saint Mary's College band in the early 1920s.

Recruiting letter and advertisements in 1925.

Saint Mary's College
TERRACE HEIGHTS
Winona, Minnesota

Office of Administration

Member of the Winona Association of Commerce

June 30, 1925

Dear Alumnus:

The Best Small College in the Northwest

We have it--your success and the success of the hundreds of other alumni have proved that St. Mary's is supreme scholastically! When Coach Skemp's warriors launched their tremendous offensive to crush the Purple and Gray of St. Thomas last Thanksgiving, they proved St. Mary's supreme athletically!

The "BIGGEST" Small College in the Northwest

You with your loyalty and with your love for your Alma Mater are going to devote a little time and a little energy--it won't take much--to bring to reality our dream--Saint Mary's, the "Biggest" Small College in the Northwest. Athletics--we don't need to worry! Coach Skemp has promised to lick Marquette and Ripon this year if you will do your share--send one student to St. Mary's.

The Plan

This is it: Formerly, the alumni were asked to submit the names of several prospective students. The results were good. But they are going to be better this year. Just submit the name of one prospect and then keep after him until you see him sign an application blank and board the train for Saint Mary's. You can convince him that St. Mary's is the Best Small College in the Northwest and he will thank his lucky stars that you were so persistent in winning him for St. Mary's.

There are young men in your community of the calibre demanded by St. Mary's. Look around, - pick one out, - put his name on the enclosed card, return the card to us at once, - and then TALK TO HIM. Keep at him, keep hammering, point out the distinctive advantages of St. Mary's--high standards of instruction, scholarship, individual attention, low expenses, athletics and music. We will correspond with him and between the two of us he will have to be convinced.

Think of Homecoming Day, when Coach Skemp makes good his promise! - Won't you be glad when you see your Alma Mater smashing on to victory over Ripon that you were one of the factors that made St. Mary's what she is--The "BIGGEST" SMALL COLLEGE IN THE NORTHWEST--Your College?

Send in that ONE name today.

Very sincerely yours,

JJW:ND

Secretary

WINONA, gateway of Minnesota's scenic wonderland, nestled in the midst of the beautiful WE-NO-NAH HILLS with their riotously colorful sentinel bluffs, caressed by the romantic Mississippi. Served by five great railroads, the Mississippi waterway, and wonderful SUNSET DRIVE, she intrigues yet satisfies every desire—rest, sport, play, or work, commerce or industry. Come to the "Heart of the Land of Golden Promise"—WINONA.

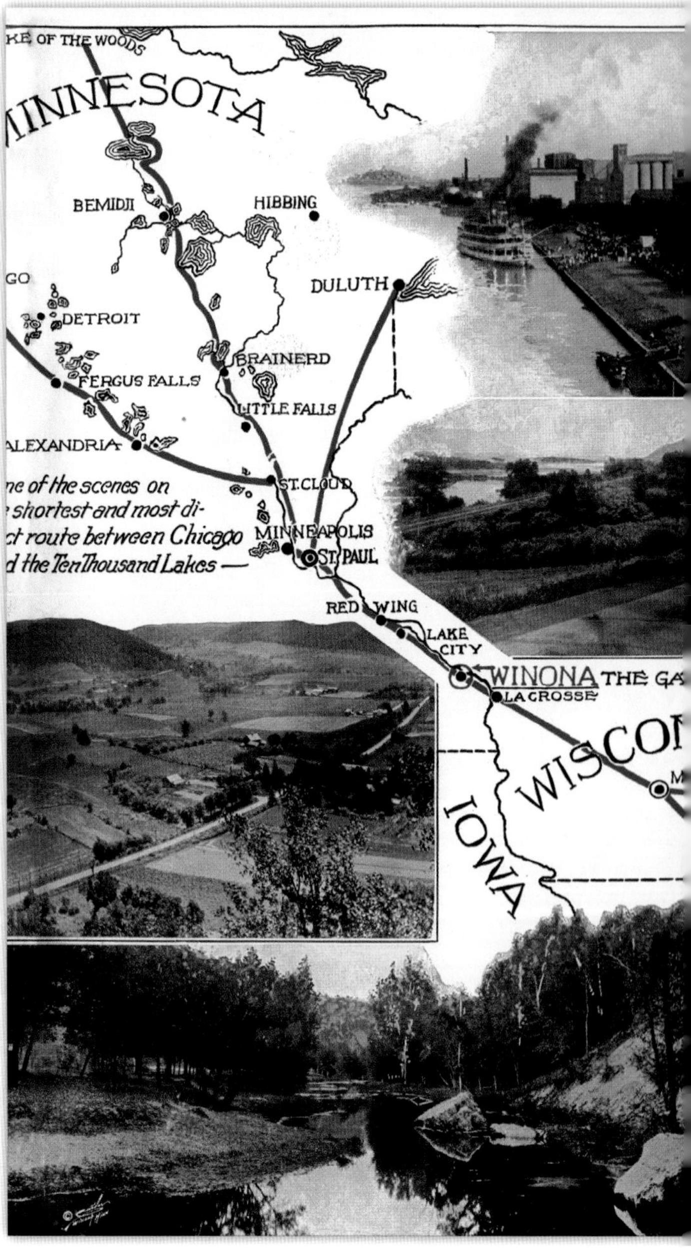

A. J. Minnaert, professor of music, 1926.

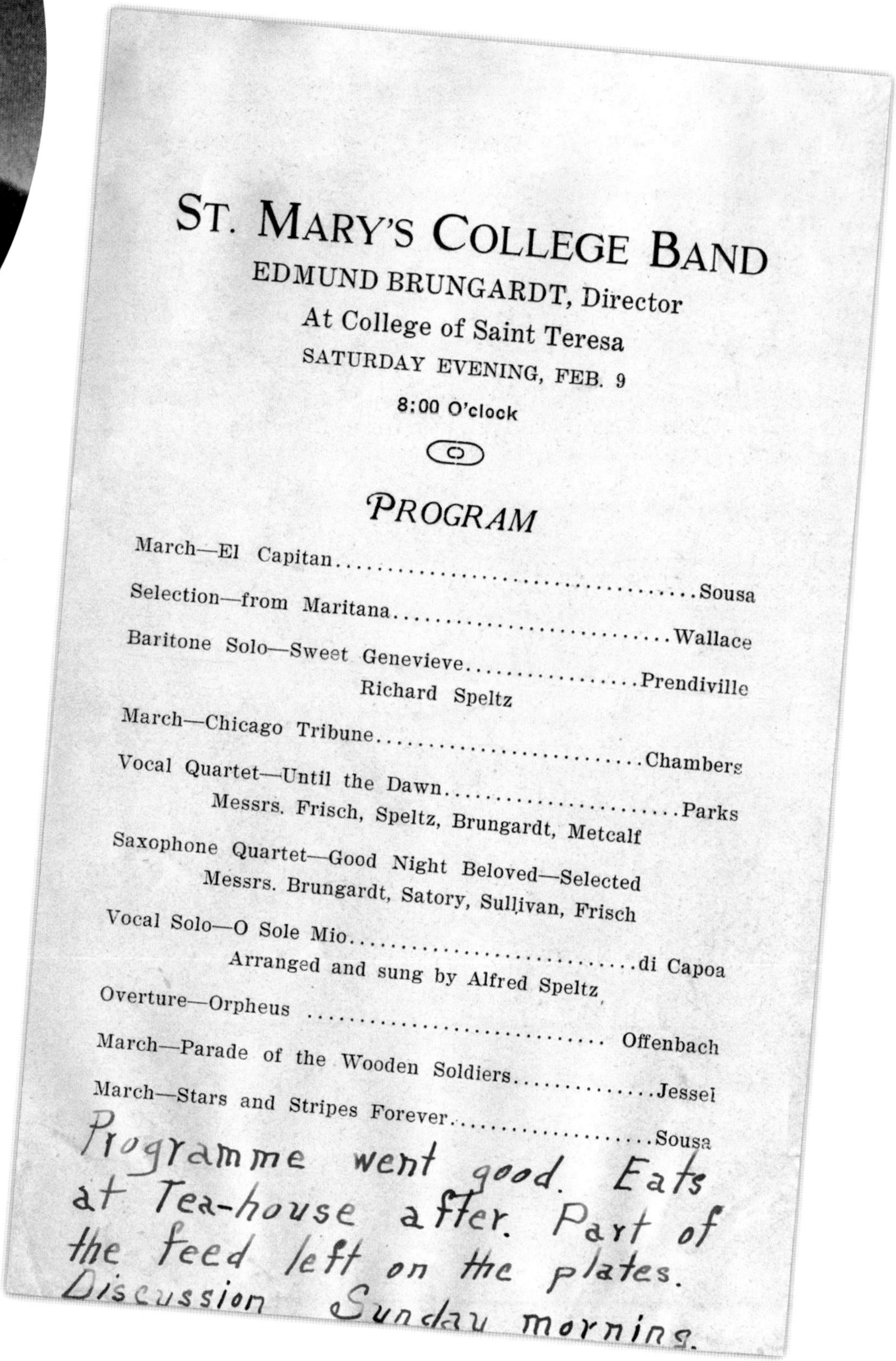

ST. MARY'S COLLEGE BAND
EDMUND BRUNGARDT, Director
At College of Saint Teresa
SATURDAY EVENING, FEB. 9
8:00 O'clock

PROGRAM

March—El Capitan.................................Sousa
Selection—from Maritana.........................Wallace
Baritone Solo—Sweet Genevieve................Prendiville
Richard Speltz
March—Chicago Tribune.........................Chambers
Vocal Quartet—Until the Dawn....................Parks
Messrs. Frisch, Speltz, Brungardt, Metcalf
Saxophone Quartet—Good Night Beloved—Selected
Messrs. Brungardt, Satory, Sullivan, Frisch
Vocal Solo—O Sole Mio..........................di Capoa
Arranged and sung by Alfred Speltz
Overture—Orpheus ....Offenbach
March—Parade of the Wooden Soldiers.............Jessel
March—Stars and Stripes Forever..................Sousa

Programme went good. Eats at Tea-house after. Part of the feed left on the plates. Discussion Sunday morning.

The program for a band concert in 1924. Soloist Alfred Speltz became the band director a few years later.

The old Beck Brewery in 1923, across Highway 14.

Ken Anderson with his banjo in a music studio in 1923.

Two Buicks and a Dodge were used by recruiters in 1923.

A 1923 winter scene at Saint Mary's College.

A fragment of a photo of faculty members in 1924.

Saint Mary's Hall in 1924, fronted by plantings and a lily pond tended by Father Julius Haun.

Coach Tom Skemp (far left) with four captains of Saint Mary's College teams, 1925.

Since the 1920s, students have climbed the nearby bluffs in all seasons.

Dr. John J. Hoffman, a Saint Mary's College faculty member from 1920 to 1962, advised a student in the chemistry laboratory in Saint Mary's Hall in the 1920s.

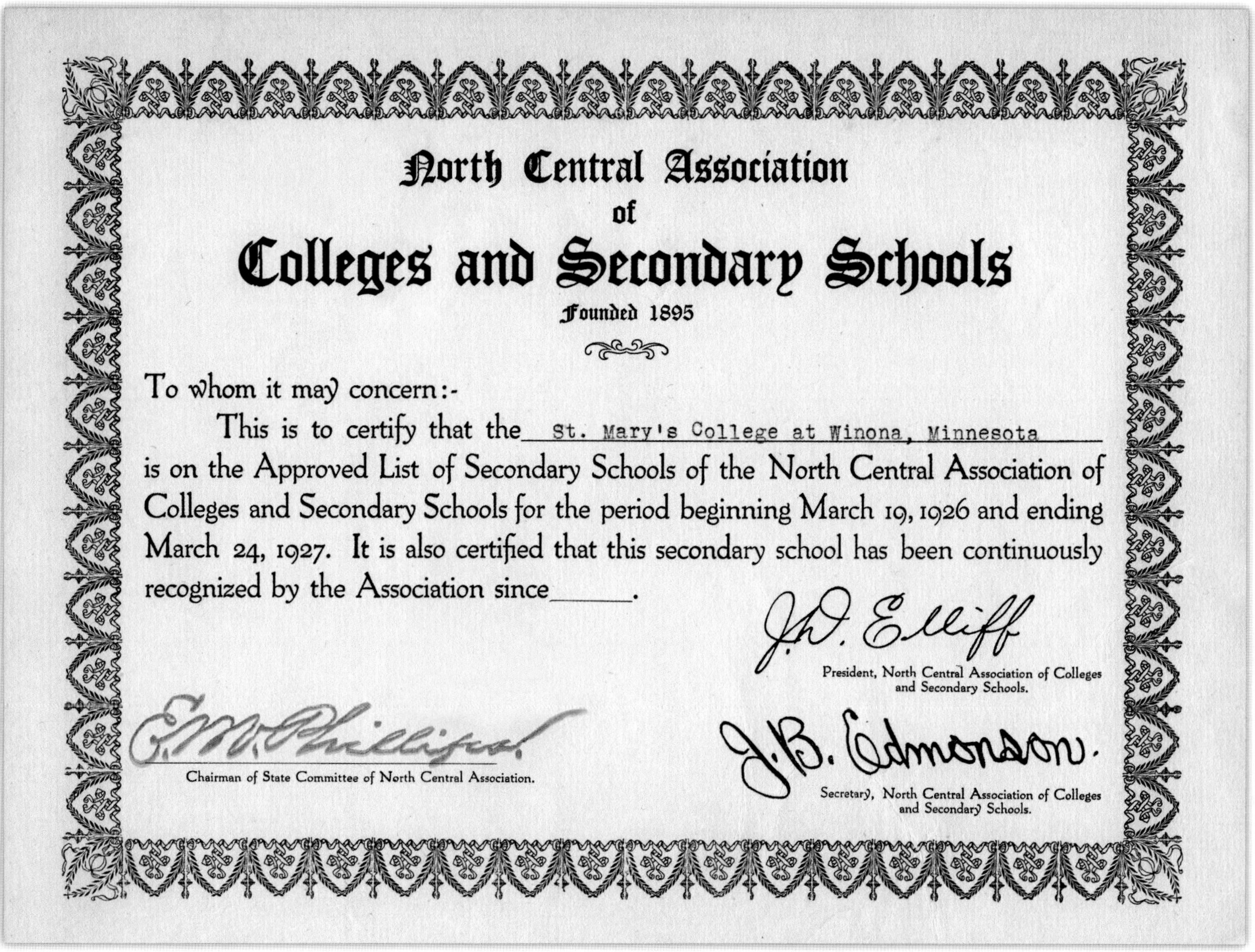

North Central Association
of
Colleges and Secondary Schools
Founded 1895

To whom it may concern:-

This is to certify that the St. Mary's College at Winona, Minnesota is on the Approved List of Secondary Schools of the North Central Association of Colleges and Secondary Schools for the period beginning March 19, 1926 and ending March 24, 1927. It is also certified that this secondary school has been continuously recognized by the Association since______.

J.D. Elliff
President, North Central Association of Colleges and Secondary Schools.

E.M. Phillips
Chairman of State Committee of North Central Association.

J.B. Edmonson.
Secretary, North Central Association of Colleges and Secondary Schools.

Professor John Gruber is shown in this 1926 photo. He later earned a doctorate at the University of California and returned to Saint Mary's College to teach History and Economics.

Four Saint Mary's College debaters in 1928.

Inter-Collegiate Debate

College Auditorium

ST. MARY'S COLLEGE

Winona, Minnesota

COLLEGE OF ST. THOMAS

vs.

ST. MARY'S COLLEGE

Tuesday Evening, March 13, 1928, at 8:30 p. m.

Affirmative	**Negative**
Lloyd Kegan, St. Thomas	George Smith, St. Mary's
Carmi Laurence, St. Thomas	Cecil Manahan, St. Mary's
Daniel F. McLaughlin, St. Thomas	Leland Darin, St. Mary's

Judges

Mr. M. A. Fraher, former Grand Knight, Knights of Columbus.

Mr. Glen E. Fishbaugher, Professor of Speech, Winona State Teachers' College.

Mr. Leo F. Murphy, Attorney at Law

RESOLVED: That the United States should cease to protect by armed forces American investments in foreign countries, except after formal declaration of war.

Saint Mary's College students in winter.

Father Ambrose McGreevey introduced hockey in the early 1920s, but not until 1928 did Saint Mary's College have an intercollegiate varsity hockey team. The 1928 and 1929 teams, pictured here with Father McHugh and Coach Karnes, were stocked with Twin Cities and Iron Range players and won consecutive state championships. The 1930–31 team compiled a 9-1 record under Coach Fred T. Robertson, losing only at Yale, and played a semi-pro team at Madison Square Garden. The 1932–33 team barnstormed up and down the East Coast.

A 1928 Saint Mary's College football game on an unidentified field.

SKEMP AND HIS MEN

A bundle of nerves in spikes and knickers,
Polishing linemen, admonishing kickers,
Showing 'em how, and where, and when,
Shake hands with the coach, Tom Skemp—and his men!

A cold wet day on the shank o' Fall,
Blocking and charging, and hawking the ball,
Just a week day grind; there's no glory then,
No frantic cheering for Skemp and his men.

The weeks roll around to Thanksgiving Day,
The Redmen kick off to the Purple and Gray!
No luck through the line, no gain round the end,
The ball's going over to Skemp's fighting men!

The old grads forget the passing of years.
There's a lump in the throat; they wink back the tears,
Where they once cheered for Riley, Roll, Toby, and Glynn,
Now their prayers and their hopes are for Skemp and his men.

Cardinal backs on a sweeping play;
The cardinal line in a bloody melee.
A punch through the line—there goes Miller again!
Give a great big hand to Skemp and his men!

—Rev. Webster L. Kenning, '22.

An early science lab in Saint Mary's Hall.

The 1927 choir.

A group of students looking stylish in the early days.

Tony Prelesnik, shown here in 1928 in his football uniform, was the oldest of three brothers from Eveleth, Minnesota. He played left wing and center for Saint Mary's College during its first two hockey seasons. He was All-American in his senior year, scoring 31 of the team's 54 goals, including eight in one game. Prelesnik played two years of professional hockey with the Chicago Shamrocks following his 1931 graduation. His younger brothers, Lewie and Ed, had outstanding athletic careers at Saint Mary's College.

Oscar Almquist, from Eveleth, Minnesota, played varsity hockey at Saint Mary's for four years and professional hockey for much of the 1930s with the Eveleth Rangers of the Central League and the St. Paul Saints of the American Hockey Association. Almquist coached high school hockey in 1937 in Williams, Minnesota, and in Roseau, where the Rams dominated Minnesota high school hockey. He coached there from 1941 to 1967, winning state titles in 1946, 1958, 1959, and 1961. The Minnesota Hockey Coaches Association has an award named for Oscar Almquist.

Oscar Almquist, All-American Goalie Selection 1932,
Captain St. Mary's Hockey Team.

THE NEXUS—
A Bond Between
Alumni and College

The Nexus

Sec. 435½, P. L. & R.
U. S. Postage Paid
Permit No. 56
Winona, Minn.

Vol. XVIII — ST. MARY'S COLLEGE, WINONA, MINNESOTA, SEPTEMBER 28, 1931 — No. 1

ST. MARY'S 7; MONTANA STATE 7

FATHER McHUGH CRASH VICTIM

Rev. Lawrence J. McHugh one of the most loved members of the faculty of the college was a victim during the past summer of an airplane crash believed to be the worst in the history of flying in the northwest.

The crash occurred on the evening of July 24 at Cass Lake, in northern Minnesota after the pilot, seeing that the plane was losing altitude as it swung low, zoomed it upward and a wing crumpled. The plane turned over and fell upside down directly in front of a group of cottagers who were waving to the occupants of the plane. The pilot apparently saw that the plane was doomed to crash as the engine was shut off and the plane did not burn after the crash. Following the inquest, Conrad, the pilot, was held blameless for the accident as witnesses claimed they distinctly heard the wing snap as the plane roared over the treetops.

The five members of the fatal party included Rev. J. J. Stapleton of Waseca, a lifelong friend of Father McHugh and also a priest of the Winona diocese. The others killed were Arthur B. Conrad, pilot; Dr. Charles C. Gault, a prominent Owatonna physician; and Ralph Ausk, ten year old son of one of Dr. Gault's

FATHER McHUGH

Father McHugh entered St. Mary's College as a student in September, 1913, and remained until 1919, after taking a complete four year high school course, and two years of college work. He then spent two years at Marquette University studying law, and there decided to study for the priesthood, going to Rome in 1922 where

Huennekens Stars as Redmen Sweep Up and Down Montana's Field For Three Quarters

LARRY SEAMAN DIES SUDDENLY

On June 4, of this year Ralph Seaman, known to us as Larry, died of a ruptured appendix, at St. Josephs Hospital in Flint, Michigan.

Larry played football at St. Mary's for four years and was one of the most brilliant and conscientious men to ever don a Redman suit. In 1927 he was elected co-captain of the team and in 1928 he was made captain. In 1929, when St. Mary's put out its best football team Larry was a mainstay. It was a revelation to watch him throw his rather short pudgy body into every play and always come up with a smile. He received all-state honors in 1929 and 1930 and in the fall of 1930 Coach T. H. Skemp picked an all-Skemp team and placed Larry at right halfback.

In June 1930 he was graduated from St. Mary's with a degree of Bachelor of Science. After his graduation he went to

HAAS, HENNESSY AND ALMQUIST INJURED

A goodly number of braves, led by Chief Huennekens, left the permanent camp of the Redmen last Tuesday evening on a hunting expedition. They were out after Bobcats and they were told that these fierce, snarling denizens of the mountains were to be found along the base of the Gallatin Range in Montana. On the way they stopped off and visited the Mandans where they brewed bad medicine for the cushion-footed dwellers of the crags.

They arrived at their destination Thursday noon and set up their tepees in the limits of Bozeman, whose inhabitants have a strange respect for Bobcats and accord to them a peculiar worship. The Redmen ignored these strange people and for two days kept to themselves, going over their hunting gear and keeping their

Father Lawrence J. McHugh, the unofficial hockey coach at Saint Mary's in the late 1920s and early 1930s, enrolled in Saint Mary's College in September 1913 and completed high school and junior college. After two years at Marquette University, he went to Rome in 1922 to enter the priesthood. He returned to teach at Saint Mary's and died in a plane crash on July 24, 1931.

The 1927 May Day parade, downtown Winona.

The third-floor chapel in Saint Mary's Hall, viewed from the balcony.

A typical student room in Heffron Hall in the early 1930s.

A 1930 view of Gilmore Creek and the open land on either side.

A Representative
of
Saint Mary's College
Winona, Minnesota
A Catholic Boarding College for Men is now in Chicago

Call REVEREND W. L. KENNING
Congress Hotel for Appointment

Located on the beautiful Mississippi River. Over night from Chicago on the Milwaukee, Northwestern, and Burlington railroads. FULLY ACCREDITED. Offering B.A. and B.S. degrees. Complete preparatory COURSES for professional schools. Only High School graduates accepted.

STATE CHAMPIONSHIP Football and Hockey teams. Basketball, Baseball, Tennis and Golf. Complete new gymnasium and athletic field equipment.

A Saint Mary's College ad in the Chicago Archdiocesan newspaper, The New World, *August 8, 1930.*

Tom Skemp resigned in December 1929 as athletic director to devote more time to his La Crosse, Wisconsin law practice, but he remained head football coach. Father W. L. Kenning, a former athlete at Saint Mary's College, succeeded Skemp. In December 1932, Skemp resigned as football coach because of the increasing workload of his law practice and his service as a federal commissioner. His football teams had a record of 61-37-9 since 1919.

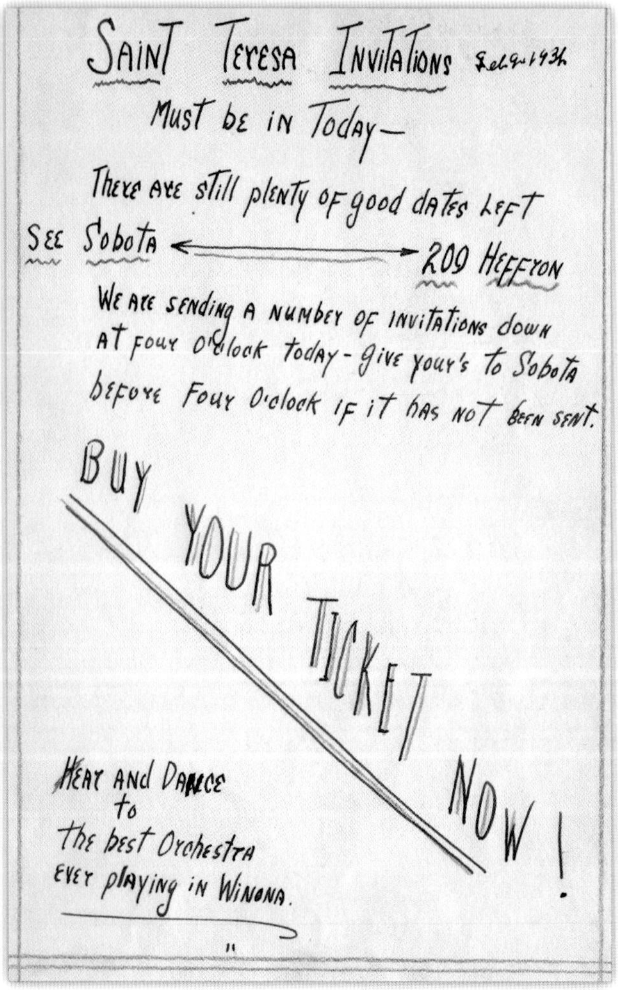

A February 9, 1931 poster invited students to a dance.

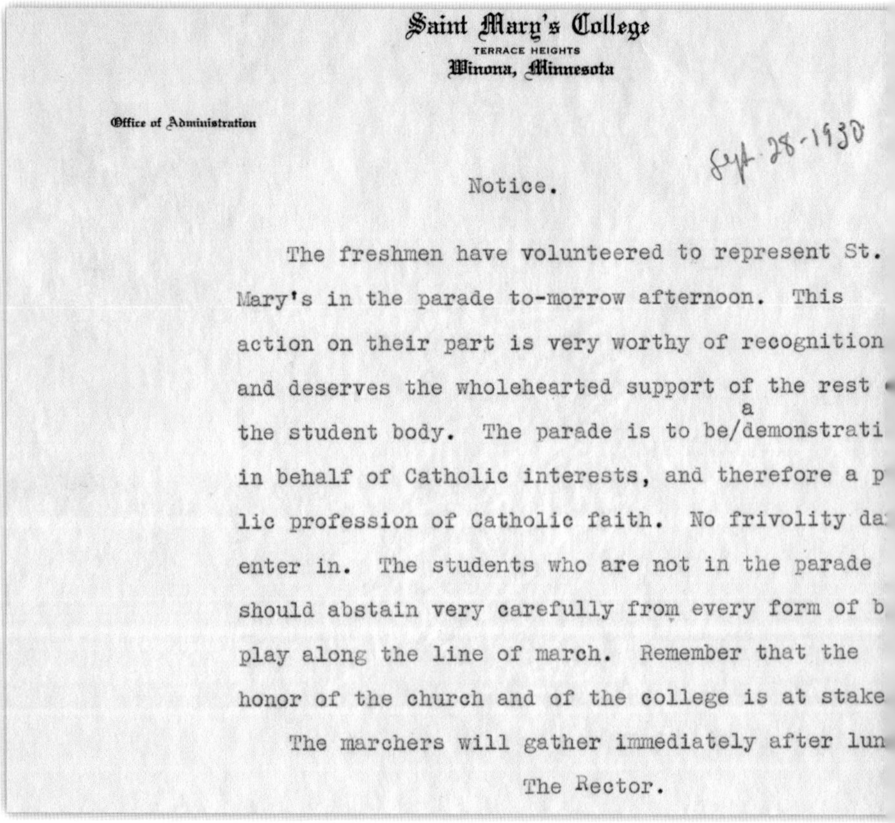

Saint Mary's College
TERRACE HEIGHTS
Winona, Minnesota

Office of Administration

Notice.

The freshmen have volunteered to represent St. Mary's in the parade to-morrow afternoon. This action on their part is very worthy of recognition and deserves the wholehearted support of the rest the student body. The parade is to be/a demonstrati in behalf of Catholic interests, and therefore a p lic profession of Catholic faith. No frivolity da enter in. The students who are not in the parade should abstain very carefully from every form of b play along the line of march. Remember that the honor of the church and of the college is at stake

The marchers will gather immediately after lun

The Rector.

The rector, Monsignor John Peschges, was a vigilant administrator.

The backfield of the 1932 football team.

Former St. Mary's Redmen

With the return of hockey to St. Mary's come memories of the days gone by. The seven men, tured above, were members of one of the greatest hockey squads in the country. Old timers will, doubt, have no trouble remembering this team of teams.

MUSTY NAMED FOOTBALL COACH

Assistant Coach Nicholas J. "Nick" Musty, a former player for Tom Skemp at Saint Mary's College and for Knute Rockne at Notre Dame, became the football coach. In the late 1930s, Musty became head football coach and athletic director at the College of St. Thomas. He became an M.D. (obstetrics-gynecology) in Minneapolis and a major and flight surgeon in the Army Air Force in World War II.

A 1933 photo of Saint Mary's College.

Chapter 2

BROTHERS: 1933–1968

The news in late March 1933 that the Diocese of Winona had sold Saint Mary's College to the St. Louis District of the De La Salle Christian Brothers came as a big surprise. But for those who were following state and national financial news that spring, the announcement perhaps was not at all surprising.

Both the city of Winona and the diocese were suffering from the financial trauma of the deepening Depression. The diocese, encompassing some of the richest farmland in Minnesota, had been struggling even before Bishop Heffron died in 1927. Much of the nation enjoyed boom times during the 1920s, but an agricultural recession plagued Minnesota and the Upper Midwest for much of that decade. Commodity prices, which fell dramatically after World War I, were just beginning to regain lost ground in 1929 when the Wall Street market collapsed.

During the next four years, the nation's farm market imploded. In the spring of 1933, Minnesota Governor Floyd Olson, the Farmer-Labor populist elected in 1930, declared a farm emergency in the state on the heels of the one-week federal bank holiday that President Franklin Delano Roosevelt declared after his inauguration in March 1932. Winona Bishop Francis M. Kelly's announcement of the sale of Saint Mary's to the Brothers came just 10 days after Roosevelt authorized solvent banks to re-open.

Minnesota's unemployment rate was nearly 25 percent in 1933. The Winona Diocese had felt the effect of the dismal financial situation for nearly six years. Shortly after becoming bishop in 1927, Bishop Francis M. Kelly notified all the parishes of the diocese's crushing debt and levied an assessment on each parish to pay it off. He assured parishioners that the diocese, not Saint Mary's College, owed the debt.

Another major problem for Bishop Kelly was the diocese's commitment to provide priests for the Saint Mary's College faculty. In 1933, he assigned 10 priests to the college, men whom he desperately needed elsewhere. In the early 1930s, his Board of Consultors had urged him to cut his losses by selling the college. Some consultors reportedly approached the Jesuits; others advised that an order of priests would not favor vocations to the diocesan clergy.

"Not if You Intend to Pay for It"

The traditional account is that the purchase of Saint Mary's College by the Christian Brothers first arose as a possibility in the summer of 1931. Since 1926, the St. Louis District had been holding its annual summer retreat on the Saint Mary's campus; an understandable choice, given the Brothers' presence at Cotter High School in Winona since 1911. The Brothers in the Cotter community had formed longstanding friendships with the priests in Winona.

The story goes that Brother Abban Philip, assistant superior general, while attending the 1931 summer retreat, asked Monsignor John Peschges, the rector, whether it would be a sin for the Brothers to covet Saint Mary's College. Monsignor Peschges, who had been advising Bishop Kelly to sell Saint Mary's, is said to have replied, "Not if you intend to pay for it."

When Brother Leopold Dodd, the provincial, returned from the summer retreat back to the St. Louis

Nine Christian Brother faculty members in the mid-1930s.

The 21 members of the Class of 1934 were the first graduates after the purchase of Saint Mary's College by the Christian Brothers.

District provincialate in Glencoe, Missouri, he reported the possibility that the district might strike a deal to purchase Saint Mary's College, a deal that could solve a thorny problem. Christian Brothers College, St. Louis, incorporated in 1855 as a degree-granting college, had burned to the ground on October 5, 1916.

The St. Louis District constructed a new building in 1921 for Christian Brothers College High School, but the need remained for a college to serve as a Scholasticate, a house of studies, for the young Brothers after their novitiate year. The only other feasible option, Christian Brothers College in Memphis, Tennessee, had phased out its college department during World War I and was now functioning only as a high school.

Since 1925, the Scholastics of the St. Louis District had been living at De La Salle Institute in Chicago, a high school the Brothers had opened in September 1892. The Scholastics took classes part-time at DePaul University and taught and lived at De La Salle Institute, a temporary solution that Brother Leopold considered unworkable over the long term. Furthermore, in 1930, DePaul University requested that the Scholastics reside on its campus as full-time students.

Late in the fall of 1931, Brother Joseph Antoninus, principal of Cotter High School in Winona since 1929, reported that Father Alfred Frisch, of the Saint Mary's Music Department, had told him that Monsignor Peschges was interested in the possible sale of Saint Mary's College to the Brothers.

After the superiors in Belgium authorized Brother Leopold to pursue the matter, he dined with Bishop Kelly on February 8, 1933, in the bishop's residence on Terrace Heights. "I came in due time and spoke to the bishop for perhaps 15 minutes without even mentioning anything about the transfer of the institution," Brother Leopold told Brother Robert Lane in 1947. "When the conversation died down, it was I who initiated the talk about the college. I said that I have heard that the diocese was willing to enter into negotiations to turn over the administration, in fact to sell Saint Mary's College to the Brothers. Then the question came up as to what return would the Brothers make to the diocese for the property, for the college. I made answer that we had no funds set aside for any such purpose at our Mother House, and that if we entered into negotiations, we would be willing to take over a debt of something like $300,000, or even slightly more, because we felt that we could pay the interest on that debt until such time as we could retire it altogether."

Bishop Kelly suggested a purchase price of $400,000. Brother Leopold countered with an offer of $325,000, with an additional $25,000 after five years if Saint Mary's College was operating sufficiently in the black for the St. Louis District to handle the increased payment. Bishop Kelly met with his Board of Consultors a week later and wrote to Brother Leopold on February 16, 1933, that they had a deal.

Brother Leopold, after receiving authorization from the District Council and from the superior general in Belgium, made a formal offer to the diocese. Bishop Kelly accepted Brother Leopold's offer and announced the agreement at an all-college assembly on March 22, 1933. The bishop felt relieved to escape $16,500 in annual debt payments, and the St. Louis District finally had its college and Scholasticate. As provincial of the St. Louis District and being near the end of his term in that office, Brother Leopold appointed himself president of Saint Mary's College.

Origin of the Scholasticate

For Brother Leopold and the Brothers, the main benefit of acquiring Saint Mary's College was the Scholasticate to prepare young Brothers academically and spiritually for their vocation as Brother and professional educator. The purchase of Saint Mary's College meant that the Scholastics would now be full-time students in a campus environment.

In 1933, students joining the Brothers came from their high schools in Chicago, Kansas City, Minneapolis, St. Paul, St. Louis, and other cities throughout the Midwest. At Saint Mary's College, the St. Louis District could operate the college and the Scholasticate with faculty and staff from its own ranks. Brother Julius Hugh, a virtual one-man university who taught the Scholastics in Chicago, joined the Saint Mary's faculty as a professor of classical languages.

When Brother Leopold announced the purchase agreement in June 1933, 19 young Brothers were already taking summer courses at Saint Mary's. Where to house these Scholastics, and the many more to follow, was the biggest problem for the Brothers in their early years of administering the college. One solution arose in the summer of 1934, when Bishop Kelly agreed to sell the bishop's residence on Terrace

Brother Leopold Julian Dodd, FSC
3rd President, 1933–1942

Brother Leopold Julian Dodd, FSC, the first Brother of the Christian Schools to serve as president of Saint Mary's College, had negotiated, as provincial of the St. Louis District, with Bishop Francis Kelly of Winona for the purchase of Saint Mary's College. Once the agreement was finalized, Brother Leopold appointed himself president of Saint Mary's College.

Born in Chicago in 1885, Brother Leopold joined the Brothers in early 1901 and taught at Christian Brothers College, Memphis, and Christian Brothers College, St. Louis, until 1914. Between 1914 and 1924, prior to his appointment as provincial, he served as principal at Cathedral High School in Duluth, Christian Brothers High School in Memphis, and Christian Brothers High School in St. Louis.

As provincial, Brother Leopold established the Superior Scholasticate residence in Chicago to provide a complete baccalaureate education for young Brothers. As the third president or rector of Saint Mary's College, Brother Leopold achieved financial stability, paid off the debt to the Winona Diocese, organized recruiting at Brothers' high schools throughout the district (especially in Chicago), and directed the successful pursuit by Saint Mary's College of academic, four-year accreditation by the North Central Association of Colleges.

Because of Brother Leopold's success at Saint Mary's, the provincial of the St. Louis District extended his term as president. In 1942, having completed his term, Brother Leopold accepted his appointment by the superior general, once again, as provincial of the St. Louis District.

Saint John Baptist de La Salle

A priest, an educational reformer, and the founder of the Brothers of the Christian Schools, John Baptist de La Salle is a saint of the Roman Catholic Church and the patron saint of teachers. He dedicated much of his life for the education of poor children in France; in doing so, he started many lasting educational practices. He is considered a pioneer of universal education.

De La Salle was born in Rheims, France, on April 30, 1651, to a family of privilege and prominence. Very early in life he felt a calling to follow a path of priesthood.

As a young man, De La Salle began working with orphan girls in the community and soon after assisted with opening a free parish school for poor boys.

These first ventures in education with underprivileged urban families became a passion that would soon consume his life and, literally, change the world of universal education.

De La Salle was astonished to find that the young men who were teaching the poorest of the poor in substandard charity schools were ill-prepared and ill-mannered and took it upon himself to inspire and educate these educators. The men lived with him in a community and worked full-time, "together and by association."

Soon after, the men began to call themselves "Brothers."

De La Salle desired all students to have equal access to education, despite their financial standing. His beliefs were ridiculed at the time. He was breaking down class barriers during a period when French society was centered on these classifications. De La Salle was determined that every student—rich or poor—would receive the same quality education, in the same classrooms, and at no cost. He recognized that education was a transformational tool that would bring individuals and families out of poverty.

At the time of De La Salle's death in 1719, there were about 100 Brothers living in some two dozen communities, conducting more than 30 schools in cities throughout France.

For his lifelong dedication and his unwavering commitment to the children he served, John Baptist de La Salle was canonized in 1900, and in 1950 he was named the patron saint of teachers.

Today, nearly 5,000 Christian Brothers—along with more than 80,000 colleagues—work together and by association in the Lasallian education mission around the world.

Heights to the St. Louis District and to move to a residence in the center of Winona. The district paid the diocese $25,000 for the former C. C. Beck home and enlarged its capacity by raising the roof to create an attic dormitory and by adding an enclosed two-story front porch.

The house built by C. C. Beck in the 1870s became the bishop's residence in 1911 and then, renamed La Salle Hall, the residence of the Brother Scholastics in 1935. When the Scholastics moved to St. Joseph Hall in 1949–1950, La Salle Hall became a student residence. Alumni who lived in La Salle Hall between 1950 and 1957 have their own stories about living during the winter in the attic and on the two front porches of the old Beck house.

When the new La Salle Hall opened nearby in 1957–1958 as the community residence for the Brothers on campus, the previous La Salle Hall was renamed Cotter Hall, in honor of the first Bishop of Winona. A small community of Sisters, Hermanas Guadalupanas de La Salle, who cooked for the Brothers' La Salle community, resided in Cotter Hall until 1971, when the Sisters moved to the third floor of La Salle Hall. From 1972 to 1989, a community of Brothers and students lived in Cotter Hall. In the ensuing years, the building was vacant and used for storage, pending its renovation to meet building code and access requirements. On June 12, 2006, a fire on the first floor of Cotter Hall, presumably set by an intruder overnight, destroyed the historic building.

In the fall of 1933, 12 more Scholastics moved to Winona from Chicago and from Glencoe, Missouri. Brother I. Philip Matthews, the future provincial of the St. Louis District, became the director of Scholastics, a position he held until 1947. He directed the formation of 180 Brothers between 1933 and 1947.

The St. Louis District purchased a two-story farmhouse across the highway from the college (known by students in later decades as the White House). Because of the cramped conditions, the Scholastics dubbed it "Heifer Hall." In 1942, Brother Justinus Elzear had acquired the Winona County Poor Farm, adjacent to the campus and beyond Heffron Hall. The building, named St. Joseph Hall, became the Scholasticate in 1948. In the 1950s, the number of Scholastics was as high as 120 annually. Brother J. Gregory Robertson, future president of Saint Mary's, was the director of Scholastics from 1947 to 1952.

Brother Leopold Dodd, the first Brother president, had a special place in his heart for the Scholastics. They received a strong foundation in religious formation alongside rigorous academic courses in Latin, Philosophy, English, History, Chemistry, Mathematics, Catechetics, Biology, Greek, Library Science, and practice teaching. The other students at the college recognized "the geese" by their long black robes and white rabat collars as they walked, often in groups, back and forth to Saint Mary's Hall. The Scholastics also had a reputation as "curve breakers."

Recruitment and Accreditation

The second advantage the St. Louis District had in operating Saint Mary's College was its network of 14 Lasallian high schools. The Winona Diocese had struggled with attracting students, mostly from southern Minnesota and western Wisconsin. Enrollment had been on a seesaw ever since the Wall Street collapse in 1929. Freshman enrollment had spiked to 127 in 1932, but the cost of college proved too high for many families in the diocese. The freshman class that entered in fall 1932 had a dropout rate of almost 50 percent the first year.

Because of the Depression, the incoming freshman class in 1933 was the smallest since the early 1920s; only 66 students enrolled, or two-thirds of the average of 100 freshmen who had enrolled annually between 1929 and 1932. The addition of Scholastics raised freshman enrollment to 102 in 1934 and 101 in 1935, but it fell to 80 in 1936.

The St. Louis District's high school-to-college pipeline grew more effective over the years. Brother Hugh Elzear, the chief recruiter for Saint Mary's College for 30 years, told a 1936 recruiters' meeting on the Winona campus that getting the high school boys to visit Winona was only half the battle. "The other 50 percent consists in visiting homes and cultivating the acquaintance of the boys' parents. The chief cause of our failure to get students is attributable to that, I believe."

A significant milestone was achieved in the spring of 1937, when the North Central Association of Colleges and Secondary Schools recognized Saint Mary's College as a degree-granting institution. "The unqualified approval of the nation's foremost educators is a signal tribute to the high standards of scholarship and adequate facilities of Saint Mary's," *The Nexus* reported.

Accreditation brought immediate benefits. In 1937, the opening enrollment at Saint Mary's was 287 students, the largest in its history. Enrollment topped 300 for the first time in 1938, and the total was 328 in 1939. Saint Mary's College was also retaining a higher percentage of students. In 1939, 92 of the 147 students who had enrolled as freshmen the previous year returned as sophomores. Enrollment held steady at an average 330 students in the early 1940s.

The Brothers fulfilled their financial obligations to the diocese and educated the next generation of their members. When Saint Mary's celebrated its silver jubilee in December 1938, Brother Leopold, the president, pledged to foster its growth and to obtain a faculty superior to any similar college or university in the Midwest.

The arrival of the Christian Brothers and the establishment of their Scholasticate at Saint Mary's College significantly changed the on-campus residential pattern. The 1940 federal census, April 10, 1940, lists 22 faculty members, almost all of them Christian Brothers assigned to Saint Mary's College by the St. Louis District, and 49 Scholastics, student Brothers between 19 and 24 years old who lived in La Salle Hall (once the Beck house and then the bishop's residence) and the White House across Highway 14.

Three priests of the Winona Diocese lived on campus: Father Julius Haun, distinguished professor from the outset and to the end of his career; Father Max Satory; and Father Bernard Mangan. Mary E. Gorman, the nurse, lived in an apartment near the college clinic in Saint Mary's Hall. Robert Woods, professor of accounting and business, lived in Heffron Hall and taught during his entire career at Saint Mary's College. Thomas Borlins, the assistant coach, also lived on campus.

The 1940 federal census also lists as residents at Saint Mary's College the eight Sisters in domestic service (bakery, kitchen, laundry, cleaning), including Sister Teresa, whose name appears on the 1920, 1930, and 1940 census

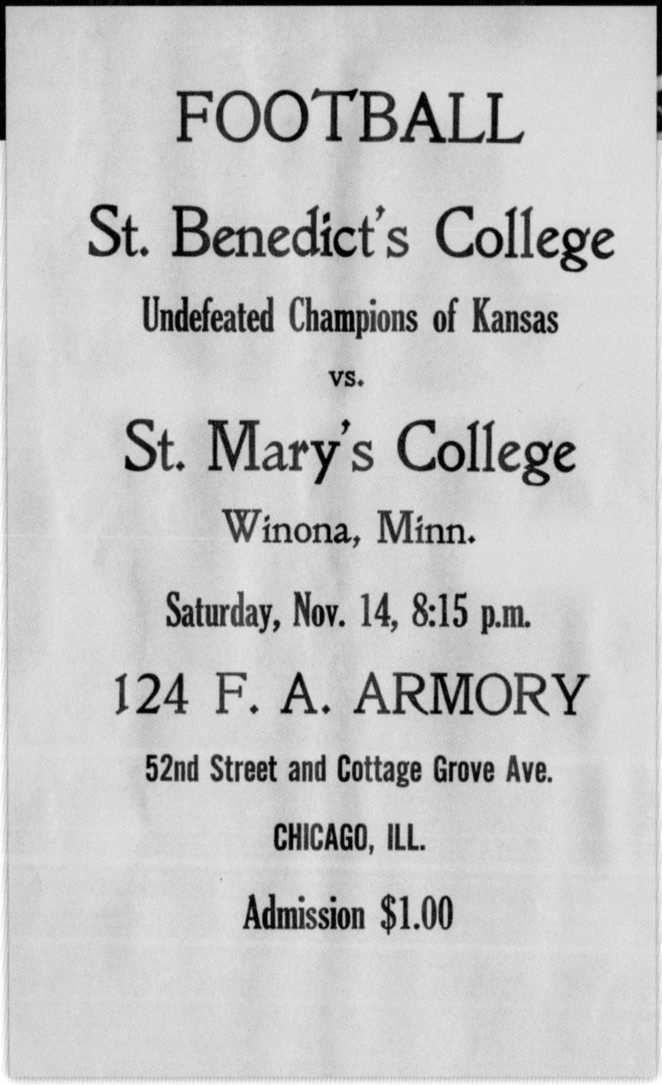

In 1936, Moose Krause (center) brought the Saint Mary's College basketball team to Chicago, his hometown.

lists. Seven other Sisters were in the community: Ermalinda, Joselle, Laurentina, Marian, Mary Evelyn, Rose Ann, and Sienna. Other employees listed as living on campus are nine single women, ages 17 to 22, working as waitresses; the boiler room engineer and his wife; one office clerk; and three farmhands.

World War II and the V-12 Program

The early 1940s were golden years for Saint Mary's College. For example, in athletics the basketball team was among the best in the region in 1939 and 1940, and former Redman standout Max Molock returned to his alma mater to coach baseball.

Perhaps the war that was raging overseas was responsible for the interest of many students in learning how to fly. Since 1938, students had been taking flying lessons, and in 1940, 30 students, nearly 10 percent of the enrollment, were taking flying lessons in the Civil Aeronautics Authority (CAA) flight training program at the Winona airport. Max Conrad, Winona's record-setting "Flying Grandfather," who had attended SMU, took a personal interest in teaching students how to fly.

Many transferred those skills to flying military aircraft after Pearl Harbor.

The Japanese sneak attack on Pearl Harbor on December 7, 1941, brought an end to 23 years of peace. The Saint Mary's alumni office kept busy changing addresses for the hundreds of alumni who volunteered for military service. In the spring of 1942, the college participated in the Victory Book Campaign of the United Services Organization (USO) to provide reading material for U.S. Army and Navy centers throughout the country. Students took part in the first scrap metal drive in Winona in what became a regular occurrence during the next four years. The cafeteria staff became used to federal rationing of coffee, sugar, cooking oil, meat, and dozens of wartime commodities.

In April 1942, the U.S. Navy Department decided to establish a V-5 Officer Training Program at Saint Mary's College, a forerunner to the later V-12 program. The V-5 program lasted three semesters and led to a commission and further training. In September 1942, the first 10 second-class seamen arrived on campus for V-5 training.

The Terrace Heights News in the fall of 1942 devoted much space to reporting on alumni who had joined the service: where they were and what they were doing. The paper also kept alumni informed of campus activities, including the 1942 retirement of Brother Leopold as president and the arrival of his successor, Brother Jerome Foy, who, like Brother Leopold, was a former provincial. The two Brothers switched places; Brother Leopold returned to Glencoe, Missouri, as provincial.

Brother Jerome spent less than two years at Saint Mary's College during years that were crucial to its survival during the war. When he realized how much the enlistments and the Selective Service draft would curtail the enrollment, he authorized Brother Hugh Elzear and Brother Joel Nelson, who would serve as president from 1943 to 1950, to contact the U.S. Navy about expanding the current V-5 program on campus. Instead, the Navy decided to include Saint Mary's College in its new V-12 program, which enrolled students in four semesters of college, with no breaks in between. V-12 students at Saint Mary's College and at 130 other U.S. colleges and universities took rigorous courses in mathematics and engineering and did military training in addition.

The first V-12 students arrived on campus in July 1943. To accommodate the Navy, Saint Mary's College adopted a year-round, three-semester schedule, beginning in July, November, and March. About 335 officer candidates enrolled at Saint Mary's College in the first year of the V-12 program. In the 1943, 1944, and 1945 academic years, average V-12 enrollment was

Opportunities for Winter Sports Abound at St. Mary's

In the St. Mary's College Infirmary and in the College Dispensar too, the seasonal illnesses and injuries are attended by Dr. Frederic Skemp, college physician, and by Miss Adelaide Des Marais, R.N college nurse.

Two cartoons from the mid-1930s in The Nexus.

Brother Landrick Jerome Foy, FSC
4th President, 1942–1943

Brother Landrick Jerome Foy, FSC succeeded Brother Leopold twice, first as provincial of the St. Louis District, and second as president of Saint Mary's College. A dedicated professional educator, the fourth president of Saint Mary's College viewed the college as a logical extension of the Christian Brothers' high schools, which were thriving throughout the St. Louis District.

In 1936, Brother Jerome, as provincial, wrote to the Brother principals of all the high schools in the district to urge them to recruit students for Saint Mary's College. "Your influence with your seniors will enable you to encourage them to plan on continuing their education at our college next September."

A St. Louis native, Brother Jerome held advanced degrees from the University of Chicago and from DePaul University. He also studied in Europe. During his career, he taught in St. Paul and Winona, Minnesota; in Chicago, Illinois; and in St. Louis, St. Joseph, and Glencoe, Missouri.

Brother Jerome was president when the U.S. Navy selected Saint Mary's College as one of 131 U.S. colleges and universities to participate in the V-12 Officer Training Program. Because Brother Jerome was ill during much of his time in office, Brother Hugh Elzear and Brother Joel Nelson were primarily responsible for the successful negotiations and administration of the V-12 program. Brother Jerome presided during an arduous time of declining enrollment in the early years of World War II. His tenure as the fourth president of Saint Mary's College was a brief one; an illness led to his death in February 1944.

285. The Brother Scholastics, exempt from military service, increased the college's enrollment during the war years. Faculty and Scholastics remember seeing the V-12 contingent on the field for 6:30 a.m. drill every day. Because V-12 students did not graduate in the traditional sense, the Class of 1945 at Saint Mary's College was a small one, 24 Brothers and two deferred civilian students.

The end of the war in August 1945 brought a rapid end to the Navy V-12 program. The last group departed in November 1945. Many U.S. Navy alumni of Saint Mary's College went on to successful careers in the military, in business, and in public life. The most illustrious graduate of the V-12 program at Saint Mary's College was Melvin Laird, Wisconsin congressman and President Richard M. Nixon's secretary of defense. According to Navy sources, the V-12 unit at Saint Mary's College ranked second among all the units in the country.

Postwar Boom

With the end of the V-12 program, the Saint Mary's administration and faculty worried about the effect on postwar enrollment. As for facilities, the Navy had trucked in three wooden structures to the Saint Mary's campus: Rooney and Ditter Barracks (battered and beloved dorms for decades later, named in honor of two Saint Mary's alumni killed in the war) and the Union, previously the Officers' Club at the U.S. Army Air Corps base in Sioux City, Iowa.

The Saint Mary's College Board of Trustees implemented a plan in the summer of 1945 to accept high school juniors for the 1945–46 academic year. In the fall of 1945, the college accepted 100 students who had completed their junior year in high school, and with the last 100 V-12 students, some returning veterans, and the Brother Scholastics, enrollment reached more than 300 students.

The floodgates opened the following year. The Servicemen's Readjustment Act of 1944, better known as the G.I. Bill, with its education benefits, motivated many veterans to obtain a college degree. So many veterans enrolled in 1946 and 1947 that Saint Mary's College installed bunk beds in the single rooms of Heffron Hall to handle the influx. In September 1947, enrollment topped 500 for the first time. With the exception of a slight decline to 487 in September 1948, enrollment at Saint Mary's never again dipped below 500.

In 1947, veterans accounted for 58 percent of the student body; most were attending Saint Mary's on the G.I. Bill. Never again would the percentage of veterans be as high, but the returning veterans laid a solid foundation for growth in the postwar period.

Classes and activities at Saint Mary's College thrived. Publication of a yearbook, the *Redman*, began in 1947. The debate team won a national competition at the College of St. Thomas in 1947. Football enjoyed a resurrection; many teams in the late 1940s had veterans who had played competitive sports in the military and were older and stronger than traditional undergraduates.

The boom in enrollment, an average between 542 and 655 students between 1950 and 1954, caused a building boom. In 1949, the St. Louis

Top Row, Left to Right — Golden, Lipinski, De Franceschi, Hnasko, Lentz, Christensen, Weide, Zannini, Lipinski.
Second Row — Kelly, Lowe, Connon, Weiler, Fale, Welsch (Capt.), Lorenz, Costello, Laurenzi.
First Row — Sheridan, O'Connor, Biesanz, Scully, Kane, Windauer, Green.

The 1935 football team, with star players Gene Zannini (top inset) and William Fale (bottom inset), had its own fight song by Francis J. McDonough:

"Saint Mary's, it's up to you.
Redmen, we're all staunch and true.
Backfield, just keep running thru
And we will winners be
(Rah! Rah! Rah!)
Fight! Fight! Fight on to the end.
Never let that old line bend;
Our honor you must defend,
So bring us victory."

First row: Sheridan, O'Connor, Biesanz, Scully, Kane, Windauer, and Green; second row: Kelly, Lowe, Connon, Weiler, Fale, Welsch (Capt.), Lorenz, Costello, and Laurenzi; top row: Golden, Lipinski, De Franceschi, Hnasko, Lentz, Christensen, Weide, Zannini, and Lipinski.

District added two wings and a third floor to St. Joseph Hall for the Scholasticate, and Saint Mary's College doubled the size of the dining hall, Griffin Hall.

In 1950, Brother Joel completed his six-year term as president and handed over his duties to his appointed successor, Brother Ambrose Groble. Two years later, Brother Ambrose announced a $1-million expansion project for the campus to add several new residence halls, a library, and a science building. The three-story science building, named in honor of the legendary professor of chemistry, Dr. John J. Hoffman, opened in 1955.

More construction occurred in the late 1950s. Brother I. Basil Rothweiler, who succeeded Brother Ambrose as president in 1956, announced in 1957 the receipt of a $760,000 Federal Housing Finance Agency loan for the construction of a student residence hall, St. Edward Hall (named in honor of the patron saint of Winona Bishop Edward Fitzgerald), and of a faculty residence, La Salle Hall, honoring the Brothers' founder, Saint John Baptist de La Salle. Since arriving on campus in 1933, the faculty Brothers, as their priest colleagues had done since the beginning, resided in two-room apartments on various floors of Saint Mary's Hall.

Saint Mary's Hall provided spaces for many purposes. For example, Brother Alphonsus Pluth, a pioneer in catechetics, moved his fledgling printing press from De La Salle High School in Minneapolis into a former laundry room in the lower level of Saint Mary's Hall in 1954. Saint Mary's College Press, as it was then known, published the *Living with Christ* series of high school religion texts. Brother Alphonsus was also the sub-director of the Scholasticate in St. Joseph Hall. When it incorporated under its own name, Saint Mary's Press moved in 1967 into a new building constructed on district property near St. Joseph Hall.

In 1958, Minnesota Governor Orville Freeman attended the groundbreaking for St. Thomas More Chapel, which replaced the 1912 third-floor chapel in Saint Mary's Hall that had become so crowded that students attended Sunday Mass in shifts. The old chapel became a large lecture hall.

One historic component of the original Saint Mary's College property burned to ashes in December

Brother Joel Stanislaus Nelson, FSC

5th President, 1943–1950

Brother Joel Stanislaus Nelson, FSC, born in Chicago, Illinois, entered the Institute of the Brothers of the Christian Schools in 1924. He made his perpetual vows during the Brothers' summer retreat at Saint Mary's College in August 1932, the year before the St. Louis District purchased it. His initial teaching assignments were at De La Salle High School, Minneapolis, 1929–1933, and De La Salle Institute, Chicago, 1933–1934. He was the director of Scholastics in Glencoe, Missouri, in 1934–1935.

Brother Joel joined the faculty of Saint Mary's College in 1938 as a teacher of Latin, after earning the Ph.D. in Classical Languages and Ancient History that year from The Catholic University of America. He already had completed bachelor's and master's degrees at DePaul University, Chicago, and in 1956, he received the master's degree in religion at the University of Notre Dame. He was also a residence hall counselor.

Brother Joel was named vice president of Saint Mary's College in August 1941 and acting president in November 1943. In March 1944, he was appointed the fifth president of Saint Mary's College. He presided over the successful administration of the 1943–1945 U.S. Navy V-12 program.

Brother Joel guided Saint Mary's College during the period of strong enrollment growth after World War II. His presidency featured the construction of the east and west wings of Saint Joseph Hall, the conversion of two wartime barracks into student apartments (Rooney and Ditter), and an addition to Griffin Hall, the campus dining hall and residence for the Sisters in charge of the food service. The Diocese of Winona opened the Immaculate Heart of Mary Seminary, Kelly Hall, during Brother Joel's term, and he fostered the unique collaboration between a minor seminary and a liberal arts college that has flourished ever since.

When his presidential term ended, Brother Joel taught at Christian Brothers College High School, Memphis, and St. Mel High School, Chicago. He returned to Saint Mary's College in August 1951 to teach Latin, Greek, and Religion and to chair the Classics Department. In 1968, he began his popular "Mind Unlimited" course, which integrated Christian principles of faith, hope, and love with the creative potential of the subconscious mind.

Brother Joel was the Brother director of the Christian Brothers community on campus from 1944 to 1950 and from 1969 to 1974.

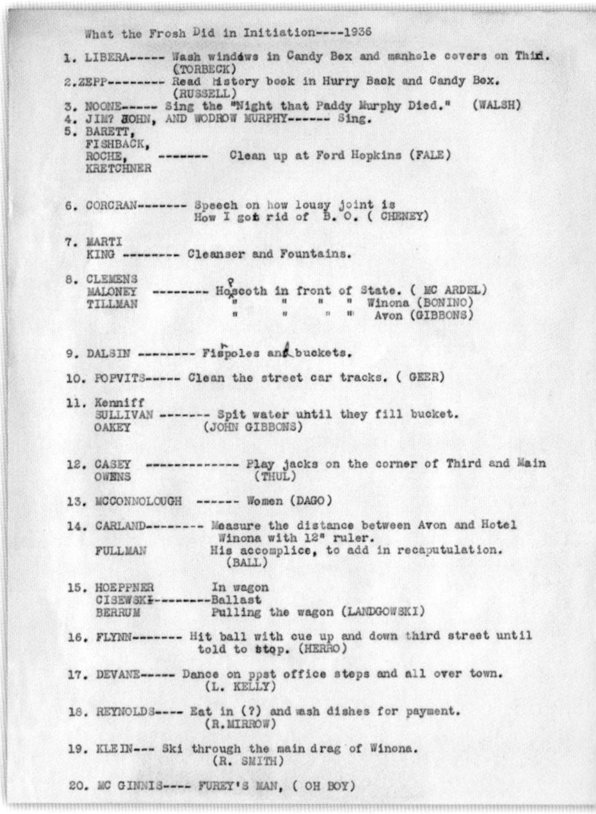

What the Frosh Did in Initiation----1936

1. LIBERA----- Wash windows in Candy Box and manhole covers on Third. (TORBECK)
2. ZEPP--------- Read History book in Hurry Back and Candy Box. (RUSSELL)
3. NOONE----- Sing the "Night that Paddy Murphy Died." (WALSH)
4. JIM? JOHN, AND WODROW MURPHY------ Sing.
5. BARETT, FISHBACK, ROCHE, KRETCHNER ------- Clean up at Ford Hopkins (FALE)
6. CORCRAN------- Speech on how lousy joint is / How I got rid of B. O. (CHENEY)
7. MARTI, KING -------- Cleanser and Fountains.
8. CLEMENS, MALONEY, TILLMAN -------- Hopscoth in front of State. (MC ARDEL) / " " " " Winona (BONINO) / " " " " Avon (GIBBONS)
9. DALSIN -------- Fishpoles and buckets.
10. POPVITS----- Clean the street car tracks. (GEER)
11. Kenniff, SULLIVAN, OAKEY ------- Spit water until they fill bucket. (JOHN GIBBONS)
12. CASEY, OWENS ------------- Play jacks on the corner of Third and Main (THUL)
13. MCCONNOLOUGH ------ Women (DAGO)
14. CARLAND-------- Measure the distance between Avon and Hotel Winona with 12" ruler. / FULLMAN His accomplice, to add in recaputulation. (BALL)
15. HOEPPNER In wagon / CISEWSKI--------Ballast / BERRUM Pulling the wagon (LANDGOWSKI)
16. FLYNN------- Hit ball with cue up and down third street until told to stop. (HERRO)
17. DEVANE----- Dance on ppst office steps and all over town. (L. KELLY)
18. REYNOLDS---- Eat in (?) and wash dishes for payment. (R.MIRROW)
19. KLEIN--- Ski through the main drag of Winona. (R. SMITH)
20. MC GINNIS---- FUREY'S MAN, (OH BOY)

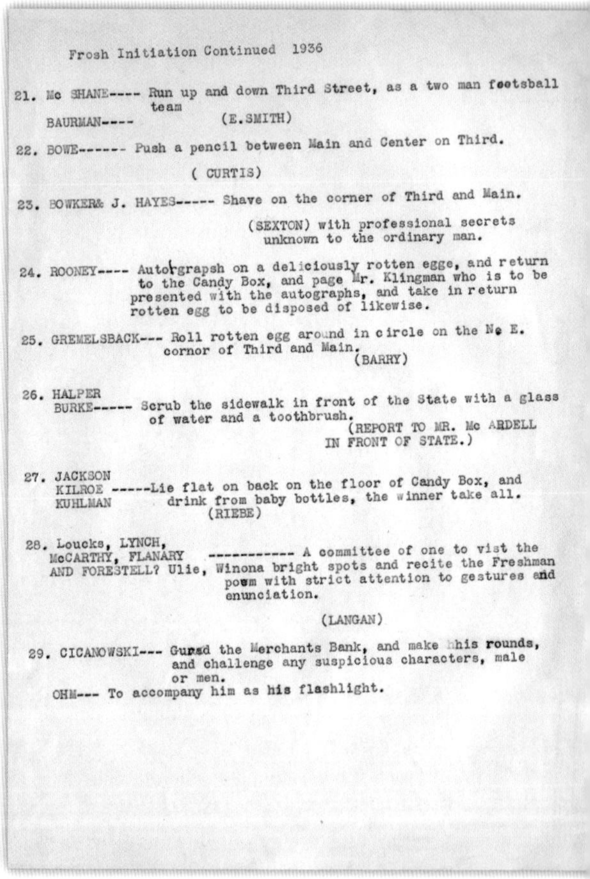

Frosh Initiation Continued 1936

21. Mc SHANE---- / BAURMAN---- Run up and down Third Street, as a two man footsball team (E.SMITH)
22. BOWE------ Push a pencil between Main and Center on Third. (CURTIS)
23. BOWKER& J. HAYES----- Shave on the corner of Third and Main. (SEXTON) with professional secrets unknown to the ordinary man.
24. ROONEY---- Autographs on a deliciously rotten egge, and return to the Candy Box, and page Mr. Klingman who is to be presented with the autographs, and take in return rotten egg to be disposed of likewise.
25. GREMELSBACK--- Roll rotten egg around in circle on the Ne E. cornor of Third and Main. (BARRY)
26. HALPER, BURKE----- Scrub the sidewalk in front of the State with a glass of water and a toothbrush. (REPORT TO MR. Mc ARDELL IN FRONT OF STATE.)
27. JACKSON, KILROE, KUHLMAN -----Lie flat on back on the floor of Candy Box, and drink from baby bottles, the winner take all. (RIEBE)
28. Loucks, LYNCH, McCARTHY, FLANARY AND FORESTELL? Ulie, ----------- A committee of one to vist the Winona bright spots and recite the Freshman poem with strict attention to gestures and enunciation. (LANGAN)
29. CICANOWSKI--- Guard the Merchants Bank, and make his rounds, and challenge any suspicious characters, male or men. / OHM--- To accompany him as his flashlight.

Task list written by sophomores for the 1936 Saint Mary's College freshman initiation.

SENIORS DON CAP AND GOWN

Vacation Edition | The Nexus | Vacation Edition

Vol. XXIII | ST. MARY'S COLLEGE, WINONA, MINNESOTA, MAY 29, 1936 | No. 6

Papal Labor Messages Reviewed

1958. A fire sparked by a backfiring tractor set farm buildings ablaze. The granary and adjacent barn were a total loss. Quick thinking by Brother Baldwin McErny helped save the college's prize herd of 90 Holstein dairy cattle.

IHM Seminary Formed

The Immaculate Heart of Mary Seminary was established by Bishop Leo Binz in 1948 adjacent to the Saint Mary's University Winona campus. Father George Speltz was appointed the first rector, with an enrollment of 25 men.

For more than 60 years, the seminary, in conjunction and collaboration with Saint Mary's, has academically and spiritually prepared the religious leaders of tomorrow. More than 1,000 men have attended the seminary since its establishment.

Student Life in the 1950s

Students could not have cars on campus in the 1950s, and the Twin Cities and Chicago were a long train ride from Winona. Back then, students rarely went home during the term. Gradually, the seniors, then the juniors, and finally all students could have a car, and parking lots sprouted on campus.

Saint Mary's College was run much the same way as when classes began in 1913. Attendance at Sunday Mass was still required, and students made an annual spiritual retreat. Lights were out each night at 10:30. The dean of men in 1961, Brother Henry Power, was an authority figure with his thick horn-rimmed glasses.

Entertainment in the days before network and cable TV and personal electronic devices consisted of intercollegiate and intramural athletics, club activities, card games in the Union, and dances and mixers with students from the College of Saint Teresa ("the Sem") and Winona State. Alumni remember "woodsies" on the nearby bluffs. At one point the championship basketball team was so popular in town that the J. R. Watkins Company of Winona loaned Saint Mary's its 16-passenger DC-3 to fly the team to some away games.

Football, however, came upon hard times. After enjoying success in the immediate postwar years, the team had a declining number of players in the early 1950s. Because fielding a team was increasingly expensive, Brother Ambrose and the administration decided to drop the sport in 1955.

The loss of football as an intercollegiate sport was balanced by the re-introduction of ice hockey in 1956. Max Molock, one of the most successful college baseball coaches in the Upper Midwest, agreed to take on the added duty of coaching the Redmen hockey team.

The 1960s

Saint Mary's College survived the Great Depression and World War II and thrived during the postwar education boom. The college was in good condition to face the challenges of the turbulent 1960s.

When Brothers who had attended Saint Mary's College in the 1940s and 1950s returned to their alma mater as faculty members in the 1960s, they found that little had changed on the Winona campus since their graduation. These alumni Brothers served the next generation of Saint Mary's students as outstanding teachers and administrators and contributed to the transformation of Saint Mary's College from the 1960s to the 1980s. Student regulations and customs changed, and a new generation's intellectual and social ferment confronted the Saint Mary's College community on its way to becoming a university community.

Saint Mary's prided itself on the high quality of the students recruited from all over the Midwest. The late 1950s and 1960s saw an academic explosion on campus as Brothers and other faculty alumni, along with teachers recruited from other colleges and universities, earned their doctorates and joined the Saint Mary's faculty and staff. Teachers were enthusiastic and well-prepared, and the focus on integration of learning encouraged all students to

Miss Clairnita Steinmetz, Queen of the Senior Ball

The queen of the Senior Ball, circa 1936.

The Saint Mary's College entrance road in 1936 ran straight to State Highway 14.

progress through a general education program, regardless of major. The strong emphasis on academic quality and the positive approach of the faculty and administration produced Saint Mary's graduates who were sought after by graduate schools in the region. The college also stressed cultural experiences and encouraged students to take advantage of seminars, guest speakers, concerts, undergraduate research, and internships.

Expansion

The postwar Baby Boom, which began around 1943, accelerated in the years following World War II, and lasted until President John F. Kennedy's election in 1960, was perhaps the major factor driving change at Saint Mary's and throughout American higher education in the 1960s. The major impact was on enrollment, which at Saint Mary's College had been climbing gradually in the 1950s, from 661 in 1955 to 861 at the end of the decade. Enrollment topped 1,000 for the first time in 1961 and averaged between 977 and 1,077 for the remainder of the decade. Enrollment in 1970 was just under 1,000; by 1979, it had climbed to 1,229.

Brother I. Basil Rothweiler, the president, reported in 1961 that Saint Mary's College was forced to turn away more than 400 applicants for the fall semester. The space crunch was so severe that the college housed 65 students in the Park Hotel in downtown Winona. The Blue Goose bus service hauled the students back and forth.

The greatest growth spurt in the college's history happened between 1955 and 1961, when enrollment jumped nearly 60 percent, just under 10 percent a year. The dramatic increase in the student body spurred a wave of building on campus. Benilde Hall, a second residence hall similar to the recently built St. Edward Hall, opened in 1960. Because of the decrease in vocations, the Congregation of the Sacred Hearts of Jesus and Mary sold Damien Hall to Saint Mary's College in 1972. Renamed later as Watters Hall in honor of Winona Bishop Loras Watters, this residence hall for 52 students included a lab theatre for the Burbage Players, a popular campus drama group.

In 1961, Fitzgerald Library, an air-conditioned facility with more than 200,000 titles, opened. Its spacious interior had seating for 425 students. During the 1970s and 1980s, Fitzgerald Library became increasingly connected by computer with other Minnesota libraries through the state's online library catalog.

St. Yon Hall, named for the community near Rouen, France, where Saint John Baptist de La Salle died in 1719, opened in 1962 in the valley across Gilmore Creek to house the Christian Brothers novitiate and the community of Brothers who administered the new Winona (St. Paul-Minneapolis) District, created from the St. Louis District because of the increasing number of Brothers. In 1968, when vocations to the brotherhood decreased markedly, the novitiate closed, and Saint Mary's College rented and later purchased the building for use as a student residence and facilities for the Music Department. A community of Brothers continued to reside in the former provincialate wing. The St. Yon valley and bluffside property occupy the former Jahnke farm, which the

St. Louis District, led by Brother Philip Matthews, purchased in the 1940s.

The housing crunch on campus was so severe in 1962 that Saint Mary's College spent $50,000 to purchase 10 mobile homes and placed them near the White House, across Highway 14. Each 55-by-10-foot mobile home housed six students.

The opening of the new gymnasium in 1965 was a red-letter day on campus. Positioned next to the baseball and softball diamonds, the soccer fields, and the intramural fields, the new gymnasium featured three basketball courts and a lower level with racquetball courts, locker rooms, training rooms, and offices.

Four years later, in 1969, the College Center (now the Michael H. Toner Student Center) opened, with a dining hall, kitchen, meeting rooms, snack bar, bookstore, mail room, Student Senate office, study lounge, and radio station KSMR-FM. The air-conditioned College Center quickly became the campus hub. The campus community bid a sad and fond adieu at the demolition of the old Union in September 1969.

The completion of the Ek Family Student Village (called the Old Village after the second village was built) in 1971 and the New Village (later named Residencia Santiago Miller) in 1973 brought to a close an intense building program. The financing for the Villages and St. Edward Hall, La Salle Hall, and Benilde Hall benefited from low-interest federal and state loans and bonds.

Under Brother Basil and Brother Gregory Robertson, who served as president from 1963 to 1969, Saint Mary's College expanded beyond anything envisioned by Bishop Heffron. In the mid-1960s, more than half of the campus facilities were less than 15 years old. Saint Mary's College had spent heavily to expand the campus, and these expenditures accumulated in a debt load that required careful management in the years ahead.

"An Electric Academic Atmosphere"

One long-time faculty member recalled the 1960s as a time of academic ferment. He recalled that the teaching skills of the Brothers and of the growing number of their talented colleagues, men and women who joined the faculty during the years of enrollment growth, permanently marked Saint Mary's College as a place where intellectual pursuits were paramount and students and faculty taught and learned side by side.

Brother Charles Severin, for example, was a prime mover in developing the pre-medicine program at Saint Mary's College. In the 1960s and 1970s, he traveled to medical schools throughout the region and asked the deans what they needed from an undergraduate pre-med program; then he incorporated their suggestions within the Saint Mary's College curriculum.

Saint Mary's College students learned to fly in the 1930s. Winona's record-setting Max Conrad was known as the "Flying Grandfather."

Another example is Brother H. Raphael Erler, who taught and advised English major Hugh Joswick, one of the 32 students in the U.S. in 1976 who were awarded the Rhodes Scholarship to Oxford University, the oldest and most celebrated international fellowship award in the world. As is typical at Saint Mary's, both student and teacher excelled.

A 1963 De La Salle High School graduate remembered seeing off friends leaving on the "Freshman Special" for Saint Mary's from Union Station in Chicago in the fall of 1963. Winona was still served by the Chicago & Northwestern, the Chicago, the Burlington & Quincy, and the Milwaukee railroads, all from Chicago, and trains were busy hauling students to and from Winona in September, over the holidays, and in May. If students wanted to go downtown or to "the Sem," they walked or took the bus. They went to see movies at the Winona Theater and the State Theater, in the same block on Johnson Street downtown. The Dairy Queen was popular with students from Saint Mary's and the College of Saint Teresa. Everyone who liked fish made it a point to eat periodically at the Hot Fish Shop on the East End.

The curriculum was heavily weighted to the arts and sciences and had been that way for years. Students took 10 to 12 courses of philosophy and theology over four years and were required to take English, Science, Mathematics, and two years of a modern language, typically French, Spanish, or German. Freshmen had to take Physical Education. Graduating seniors had to complete a bachelor's thesis to earn their degree. Saint Mary's College, however, was undergoing a significant shift from an emphasis on theology and philosophy to a new focus on the sciences, the arts, and the professions.

Brother Gregory told *The Nexus* in January 1964 that he wanted Saint Mary's to remain a small

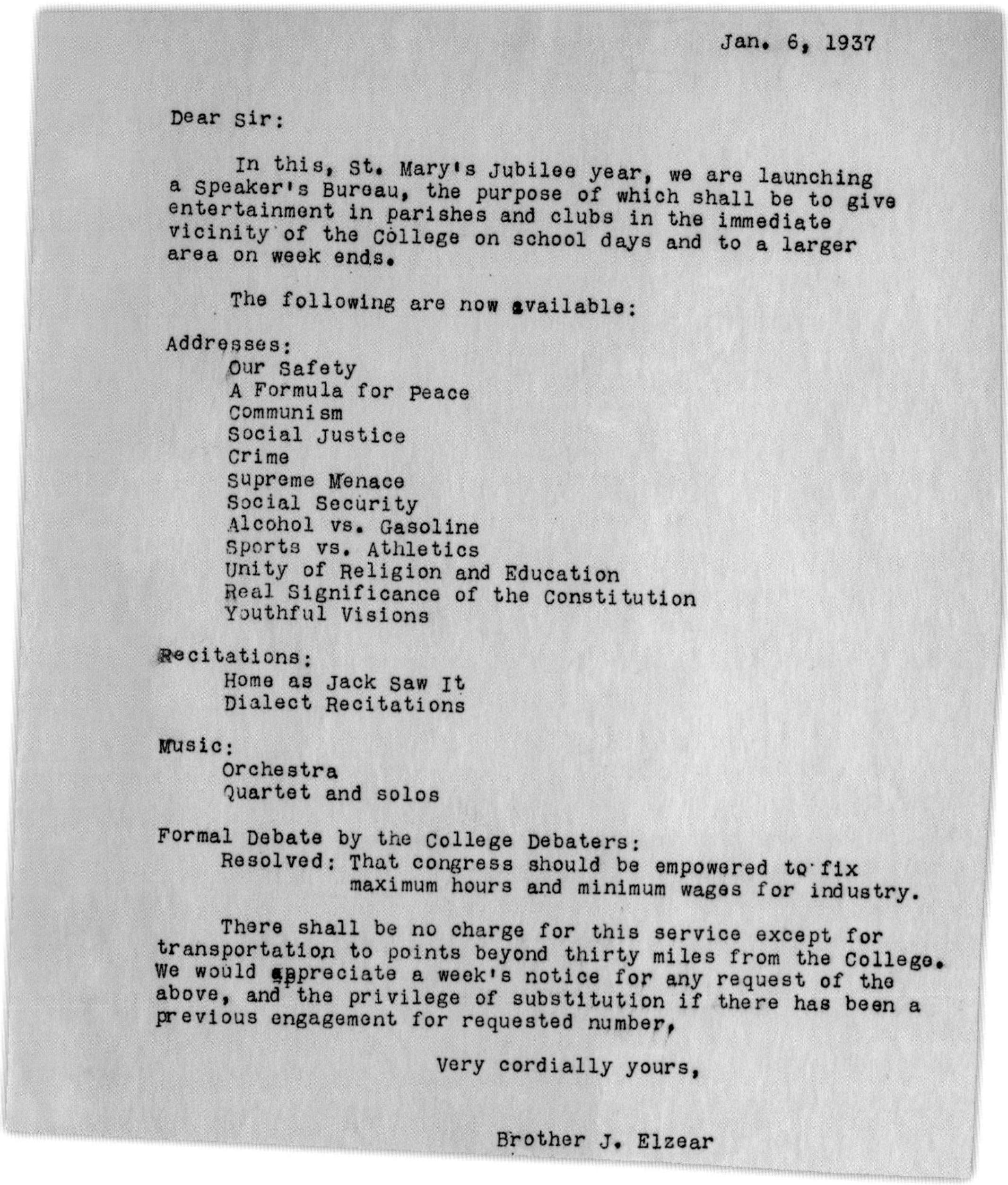

Jan. 6, 1937

Dear Sir:

In this, St. Mary's Jubilee year, we are launching a Speaker's Bureau, the purpose of which shall be to give entertainment in parishes and clubs in the immediate vicinity of the College on school days and to a larger area on week ends.

The following are now available:

Addresses:
- Our Safety
- A Formula for Peace
- Communism
- Social Justice
- Crime
- Supreme Menace
- Social Security
- Alcohol vs. Gasoline
- Sports vs. Athletics
- Unity of Religion and Education
- Real Significance of the Constitution
- Youthful Visions

Recitations:
- Home as Jack Saw It
- Dialect Recitations

Music:
- Orchestra
- Quartet and solos

Formal Debate by the College Debaters:
Resolved: That congress should be empowered to fix maximum hours and minimum wages for industry.

There shall be no charge for this service except for transportation to points beyond thirty miles from the College. We would appreciate a week's notice for any request of the above, and the privilege of substitution if there has been a previous engagement for requested number,

Very cordially yours,

Brother J. Elzear

liberal arts college. He told the student reporter that "education today demands personal, human contact within a closed society." Brother Gregory and the faculty were adapting the curriculum to allow science majors, for example, to forego certain components of the previously required curriculum.

Students at Saint Mary's College and on almost every campus in America vociferously opposed President Nixon's introduction of a draft lottery in December 1969. Dramatic social change was occurring during the coming-of-age of the Baby Boomers. Students demanded and got a voice on campus.

Hundreds of Saint Mary's College alumni served in the military, and four perished, during the Vietnam War. Some faculty and students were active in peace groups and anti-war activities on campus and in Minnesota, which with its many campuses was a focal point for the anti-war movement. Although conservative on many social and academic issues, the Brothers were strong proponents of peace and social justice.

In the late 1960s, three nationally publicized cases occurred of anti-war activists who broke into draft boards and spilled blood on files: Catonsville, Maryland; Chicago; and Milwaukee. Brother K. Basil O'Leary, head of the Economics Department, was one of the leaders of the Milwaukee 14 incident in September 1968.

When Dr. Marilyn Frost (formerly Solberg) arrived on campus for her first teaching job out of graduate school, Saint Mary's was on the cusp of dramatic change. A New York City native, she had done graduate work in psychology at the University of Wisconsin–Madison and started teaching at Saint Mary's in September 1969. She had little previous contact with the Christian Brothers or with the priests, but she was amazed by the academic rigor on the campus.

Dr. Larry Luttmers grew up in a small farm community in South Dakota and earned his undergraduate degree at the University of Minnesota–Marshall. Following graduate school at North Dakota State University in Fargo, he arrived on Saint Mary's campus in the fall of 1968. What initially impressed him the most was the esprit de corps of the faculty and staff.

Faculty from the period recalled that the decade, although one of tremendous academic rigor, was a tumultuous time, with everyone involved on all sides of the issues. They attributed the high level of intellectual pursuit and awareness of social justice issues to the Brothers, who would never allow a simple answer to a complex problem and who never hid what they believed.

One faculty member called the Brothers the gene that united the community. Another recalled Brother Julius Winkler, who had been a conservative but became a radical. Dr. Frost gave the Brothers the highest compliment: "They were always educators."

Saint Mary's College was becoming a pioneer in curriculum reform relative both to the real world after college and to the individual goals of the students. The college had adopted modular scheduling in the 1960s, a radical position at the time, and was at the forefront of the institutional development programs funded by the federal government. A comprehensive curriculum and faculty development program between 1967 and 1977, funded by Title III of the Higher Education Act of 1965, enabled Saint Mary's College to study enrollment patterns, to strengthen the curriculum, to develop information technology, and to foster faculty development in academic areas related to evolving careers and opportunities.

Brother Hugh Elzear welcomed visiting parents.

DISTRIBUTION OF GRADES BY TEACHER

Instructor	Total Grades	Percentage of: A's	B's	C's	D's	F's
1	57	17.5	24.6	35.1	12.3	10.5
2	80	23.7	47.5	28.8	0.0	0.0
3	57	7.0	42.1	29.8	12.3	8.8
4	83	7.2	36.1	42.2	10.9	3.6
5	79	0.0	39.3	45.6	10.1	5.0
	92	9.8	20.6	44.6	22.8	2.2
	54	11.1	27.8	50.0	5.6	5.5
	24	4.2	33.3	37.5	25.0	0.0
	37	2.8	27.0	35.1	27.0	8.1
	74	8.1	28.4	43.3	14.8	5.4
	23	17.4	39.1	17.4	13.1	13.0
	35	8.6	25.7	31.4	22.9	11.4
	33	24.2	30.3	36.4	9.1	0.0
	58	17.3	29.3	41.4	8.6	3.4
	61	11.5	9.9	29.5	36.1	13.0
	32	12.5	28.1	34.4	15.6	9.4
	82	11.0	34.1	45.0	3.7	6.2
	18	16.7	38.9	33.3	11.1	0.0
	73	12.3	23.3	41.1	13.7	9.6
	11	18.2	54.5	18.2	9.1	0.0
	46	[illegible]	36.9	32.6	17.4	0.0
	[illegible]	[illegible]	20.8	41.6	23.0	[illegible]
	[illegible]	[illegible]	[illegible]6.5	31.8	15.[illegible]	[illegible]

This fragment of the grade distribution by 1937 faculty at Saint Mary's College showed that as many students earn D *or* F *as earn* A *or* B.

Social Message

BY WESTERN UNION

COPYRIGHTED 1936 BY WESTERN UNION TEL. CO.

LD859 LU (AA1193) 24 NL

STLOUIS MO

BROTHER LEOPOLD DIRECTOR

3455 SOUTH WABASH AVE CHICAGO ILL

CONGRATULATIONS ON THE ACCREDITING OF STMARYS COLLEGE THE BROTHERS OF STLOUIS REJOICE WITH YOU ON THIS OCCASION MAY THE FUTURE BRING STILL GREATER SUCCESS

BROTHER HENRY DIRECTOR

THE COMPANY WILL APPRECIATE SUGGESTIONS FROM ITS PATRONS CONCERNING ITS SERVICE

CLASS OF SERVICE
This is a full-rate Telegram or Cablegram unless its deferred character is indicated by a suitable symbol above or preceding the address.

WESTERN UNION

R. B. WHITE, PRESIDENT — NEWCOMB CARLTON, CHAIRMAN OF THE BOARD — J. C. WILLEVER, FIRST VICE-PRESIDENT

SYMBOLS
DL = Day Letter
NM = Night Message
NL = Night Letter
LC = Deferred Cable
NLT = Cable Night Letter
Ship Radiogram

The filing time shown in the date line on telegrams and day letters is STANDARD TIME at point of origin. Time of receipt is STANDARD TIME at point of destination

Received at 174 Center St., Winona, Minn. Telephone No. 2312

MT27 14=STPAUL MINN 9 1032A — 1937 APR 9 AM 10 45

BROTHER JUSTUS=

STMARYS COLLEGE Winona, Minn.

THIS IS THE DAY THE LORD HATH MADE HURRAH WITH FIRE WORKS TRIUMPHANT CONGRATULATIONS=

BROTHER J MATTHEW.

1937 APR 9 TELEPHONE TO Bro. J.
TIME AM 10 53 BY
DISPOSITION Mail

WESTERN UNION ALONE SERVES 89% OF THE PLACES HAVING TELEGRAPH OFFICES

275 Harriet Street,
April 9, 1937.

My dear Brother Leopold:

Last night on my return from Saint Paul, I found your message awaiting me. I am very pleased to learn that Saint Mary's College has been admitted to membership in the North Central Association. I am grateful for your kindness in sending me the telegram.

I know how manfully you and your staff have worked to attain this recognition from the Association which is made up of so many institutions in this section of the country. There is a sense of real achievement in gaining the purpose you set out to win. You have my sincerest good wishes and congratulations.

I have been aware through all the years of the life of the College of the devoted service of the members of its faculty. When I was privileged to be a member of the body of teachers, I tried to build up fine traditions and instil in the hearts of the students a love for truth. Those who have carried on in the work both with me and after me, have labored for the same high ideals. May God keep them always high and noble.

With the attainment of your purpose comes an added responsibility. You must strive to make Saint Mary's stronger still and spread its influence for good amongst our youth.

Asking God to bless Saint Mary's,

I remain,

Sincerely in Christ,
+ Francis M. Kelly
Bishop of Winona.

Brother Leopold,
Saint Mary's College.

Father Julius W. Haun (left) and two faculty colleagues read the 1937 accreditation announcement.

Bishop Francis M. Kelly presided at a late 1930s Saint Mary's College graduation in the upper gymnasium.

The 1941 baseball team won the state championship. When Coach Moose Krause left in 1940 to be assistant football coach at Holy Cross, Saint Mary's College hired Eddie Suech as head football and basketball coach, and he hired alumnus Max Molock, an all-around athlete at Saint Mary's, as assistant football and basketball coach and head baseball coach. Seated: Jerome H. Rolen, unidentified, Mark Merkulird, Curt Youngs, Andy Kelleher, Dan Enright, Bob Banerken, Hal Cory, and Russ Maloy; standing: Max Molock, Tom Barrett, Joe Kraft, Reno Rossini, Tom DePrell, Jack Hennessey, Tony Graham, Gene Farrell, Tom Cransie, Clem Siemer, and Ed Lowe.

The program cover for the Saint Mary's College vs. Winona State College football game, Friday, September 19, 1941.

These six members of the 1941–42 basketball team also belonged to the Flying Club.

Christian Brothers on campus, 1930s.

1929

The last high school class graduates; Saint Mary's applies for accreditation as a college.

1931

The hockey team includes future All-Americans Tony Prelesnik and Oscar Almquist.

1933

The St. Louis District and Winona Bishop Francis Kelly agree to terms for the Brothers of the Christian Schools' purchase of Saint Mary's College.

Brother Leopold Julian Dodd is the first Christian Brother president of Saint Mary's College.

1934

Edward Walter "Moose" Krause, who graduated from Notre Dame in 1934 and later became athletic director there, coaches basketball at Saint Mary's from 1934 to 1939.

The student Brothers, or Scholastics, move from Chicago to Saint Mary's.

1935

Brothers recruit students to Saint Mary's from their four Chicago high schools: De La Salle, Saint George, Saint Mel, and Saint Patrick.

1936

The Great Depression continues to wreak havoc on enrollment: only 80 freshmen register for the fall term.

1937

The North Central Association of Colleges and Secondary Schools accredits Saint Mary's College as a degree-granting institution.

1938

Saint Mary's celebrates its silver jubilee.

1940

Max Molock '36, an outstanding athlete, returns to his alma mater Saint Mary's to coach baseball.

Saint Mary's joins Delta Epsilon Sigma in 1940. DES is a national scholastic honor society for students, faculty, and alumni of colleges and universities with a Catholic tradition.

1941

Japan attacks Pearl Harbor, and America is at war for the second time in a generation. Over 1,000 students and alumni are in military service during the next four years.

1942

Brother Landrick Jerome Foy succeeds Brother Leopold Dudd as president of Saint Mary's College.

1943

Brother Joel Nelson succeeds Brother Jerome Foy as president.

Saint Mary's is one of 131 colleges and universities that the U.S. Navy selects for its V-12 program to train naval officers. The first trainees arrive in July.

1944

Saint Mary's enrollment consists of 285 Navy V-12 trainees and 15 Brother Scholastics.

Congress passes the "G.I. Bill."

1945

The administration decides to accept students who have completed three years of high school; around 100 enroll.

The Navy V-12 program kept the college afloat during WWII.

1946

Saint Mary's begins publishing the college yearbook, *Redman*.

1947

Enrollment tops 500 for the first time and includes many veterans receiving G.I. Bill benefits.

The debate team wins a national competition at the College of St. Thomas in St. Paul.

1948

Bishop Leo Binz urges the people of the Winona Diocese to fund a seminary building on the Saint Mary's campus.

1950

The St. Louis District of the Brothers renovates the former Winona County Poor Farm building to serve as the Scholasticate, St. Joseph Hall.

Brother J. Ambrose Groble succeeds Brother Joel Nelson as president.

Construction of the Immaculate Heart of Mary Seminary begins.

1951

Bishop Leo Binz dedicates the Immaculate Heart of Mary Seminary, named Kelly Hall in honor of Bishop Francis M. Kelly.

Saint Mary's conducts for the first time National Science Foundation summer workshops for high school science teachers.

1952

Brother Ambrose Groble announces a $1-million capital expansion of several residence halls, a library, and a science building.

1955

Citing costs, Saint Mary's ends intercollegiate football.

Groundbreak for Aquinas Hall, 1953.

Benilde Hall after construction, 1961.

1956

Brother I. Basil Rothweiler succeeds Brother Ambrose Groble as president.

Saint Mary's reintroduces intercollegiate ice hockey.

1957

The college receives a low-interest loan of $760,000 from the Federal Housing Finance Agency to construct two residence halls, St. Edward and La Salle.

1958

Minnesota Governor Orville Freeman participates in the groundbreaking for the St. Thomas More Chapel.

Fire destroys much of the campus farm. Brother Baldwin McEnery's quick action saves the Saint Mary's herd of 90 dairy cattle.

Congress passes the National Defense Education Act, including support for loans to college students and for the improvement of science, mathematics, and foreign language instruction.

1960

Benilde Hall and St. Edward Hall accommodate the influx of resident students.

The Congregation of the Sacred Hearts of Jesus and Mary inaugurates Damien Hall Seminary, constructed on the college's former farm property across Highway 14.

1961

Enrollment tops 1,000 for the first time because of the postwar Baby Boom and Saint Mary's has to turn away 400 applicants.

Students, faculty, and staff move the library of 200,000+ volumes from Saint Mary's Hall to the new Fitzgerald Library, named in honor of Bishop Edward A. Fitzgerald.

Saint Mary's offers graduate courses for IBM employees in Rochester, Minnesota.

On the former Janhke farm across Gilmore Creek, the St. Louis District opens St. Yon Hall to house postulants and novices.

"What started as a school for boys became a top-tier national university with a global footprint"

SAINT MARY'S UNIVERSITY
Centennial Timeline

The founder,
Bishop Patrick Heffron.

1911

The Winona Board of Trade purchases and deeds to Bishop Patrick Heffron 160 acres on Terrace Heights as a site for a college for boys.

On Thanksgiving Day, Bishop Heffron dedicates Cotter High School, staffed by the Brothers of the Christian Schools at his invitation.

1912

On Memorial Day, May 30, Bishop Patrick Heffron delivers a sermon at two cornerstone ceremonies, at Saint Mary's College and at the College of Saint Teresa.

Bishop Heffron appoints Father William E. F. Griffin as rector of Saint Mary's College.

1913

Saint Mary's College welcomes 100 students when classes begin on September 27.

The student body votes to organize an athletic association so that students are eligible to compete in intercollegiate baseball, basketball, and football.

1914

In the spring, the library opens on the third floor of Saint Mary's Hall, with most books donated by faculty members.

1915

A deranged diocesan priest shoots Bishop Heffron while the bishop is saying morning Mass in his private chapel in Saint Mary's Hall. The bishop survives the assassination attempt and forgives his attacker.

Saint Mary's Hall cornerstone, May 30, 1912.

1917

The United States declares war on Imperial Germany; 50 former and current students serve in the Army, Navy, and Marine Corps during the Great War.

1919

Saint Mary's announces a major capital campaign for a second building, Heffron Hall, and a power plant.

1920

The campaign's success enables construction of Heffron Hall in the spring.

1923

Student recruitment expands beyond the Winona Diocese into neighboring areas and Chicago.

1924

The college establishes the departments of Philosophy and Education. Father Julius Haun is one of the most popular teachers.

1926

Saint Mary's awards diplomas to the initial 10 students who completed the four-year college degree.

The Minnesota Intercollegiate Athletic Conference (MIAC) admits Saint Mary's College to membership.

The Christian Brothers' St. Louis District again holds its annual summer retreat on campus.

1927

Bishop Heffron dies of cancer.

Coach Tom Skemp and the football team are undefeated in MIAC competition.

Women changed the face of campus beginning in 1969.

1962

To address the student housing shortage, Saint Mary's places 10 mobile homes on the former farm property across Highway 14.

1963

Brother Gregory Robertson succeeds Brother Basil Rothweiler as president.

1965

The new gymnasium increases the capacity and the quality of campus athletic facilities.

Congress passes the Higher Education Act, which authorizes assistance for post-secondary educational institutions and financial aid for needy college students. Saint Mary's College receives significant Title III (Aid to Developing Institutions) funds into the 1970s for development of faculty, curriculum, and computer technology.

1968

Students increasingly protest the war in Vietnam as the Tet Offensive convinces many that the war in Southeast Asia is already lost.

Hundreds of Saint Mary's students and alumni serve, and four perish, during the Vietnam War.

1969

Saint Mary's admits full-time undergraduate female students for the first time, which quickly ends a trend of declining enrollment.

The College Center opens and replaces the antiquated but memorable 1940s Army-surplus Student Union.

Brother George Pahl, a noted researcher in oncology radiation and a popular professor on campus, succeeds Brother Gregory Robertson as president.

1971

Ek Family Student Village, called the "Old Village" when the "New Village" opens a year later, is the newest housing on campus.

1976

Brother Peter Clifford succeeds Brother George Pahl as president and reinforces the link between Saint Mary's and the Winona community by serving on the boards of the Winona Chamber of Commerce and the Norwest Bank.

Hugh Joswick '76, an English major, wins a Rhodes Scholarship for postgraduate study at the University of Oxford; Brother H. Raphael Erler is his faculty advisor.

1978

Fastpitch softball becomes the first intercollegiate sport for women at Saint Mary's.

1980

Saint Mary's sets an enrollment record when 1,272 students arrive in September.

Alumnus Jan Janssen plays as a right wing for the Netherlands National Hockey Team at the Lake Placid Winter Olympics.

Brother George Pahl teaching biology.

Graduate programs in Minneapolis, 1984.

1982

Saint Mary's leases classroom space in a St. Paul union hall and in Twin Cities Christian Brothers high schools to offer graduate courses in the late afternoon and evening.

1983

The 1981–1982 recession is a factor in an enrollment of less than 1,200 students for the first time since 1976.

Saint Mary's College and Abbott Northwestern Hospital create a graduate degree program for nurse anesthetists in Minneapolis.

1984

Brother Louis DeThomasis succeeds Brother Peter Clifford as president. A financier, Brother Louis transforms Saint Mary's College during his 21 years in office.

Brother H. Charles Severin, founder of the Biology Department, celebrates his 50th year at Saint Mary's College.

1985

Saint Mary's leases the first floor of 2500 Park Avenue, Minneapolis, for classroom and office space for the growing graduate programs.

The women's soccer team finishes 19-3, wins the MIAC championship, and ranks 20th in the USA.

1987

The Performance Center's Joseph Page Theatre and Figliulo Recital Hall open.

Brother Charles Hall, a new wing, and Hoffman Hall, the original building, form the Adducci Science Center.

1988

The Christian Brothers residence opens on property owned by the Brothers' district; La Salle Hall becomes a student residence and a classroom building.

1989

The College of Saint Teresa, founded by the Rochester Franciscan Sisters as the Winona Seminary for Women in 1894, closes.

1990

Saint Mary's completes a record $12.5-million capital campaign to expand the graduate program in Minneapolis.

1992

Saint Mary's establishes Christ the Teacher Institute for Education (CTIE) at Tangaza College in Nairobi, Kenya.

1993

The Theatre Department lays the groundwork for a junior semester abroad program in London.

1994

With the opening of the Gostomski Fieldhouse and the Jul Gernes Pool, Saint Mary's has the most complete athletic facilities in the MIAC.

1995

The Higher Learning Commission of the North Central Association of Colleges and Schools accredits Saint Mary's as a university.

A new home for performing arts, 1987.

1997

Saint Mary's University of Minnesota becomes the sole administrator of the Nurse Anesthesia program and locates it at the Minneapolis Graduate Center.

2000

The women's fastpitch softball team wins the NCAA Division III national championship.

2002

Saint Mary's purchases the campus of the former College of Saint Teresa in Winona.

2003

Saint Mary's University opens its Apple Valley center in partnership with Dakota County Technical College (DCTC) and Inver Hills Community College (IHCC).

Saint Mary's inaugurates the Saint Teresa Leadership and Service Institute for Women.

2005

Brother Craig Franz succeeds Brother Louis DeThomasis as president.

2006

Cotter Hall, the former C. C. Beck home, then bishop's residence, Scholasticate, Sisters' convent, and Brother-student community, burns down on June 12.

Two programs in Nairobi extend the global reach.

2008

Brother William Mann becomes the 13th president. Brother William was the Vicar General of the Institute of the Brothers of the Christian Schools.

Saint Mary's opens its Minnetonka center to offer graduate programs to residents of the western suburbs of Minneapolis.

The new Veterans Memorial on the Winona campus honors alumni who have served in the U.S. military.

2012

Saint Mary's launches a strategic planning initiative to position itself for continued growth in its second century.

Women's fastpitch wins the national championship, 2000.

Enrollment Timeline

Saint Mary's College opened its doors on September 27, 1913, to 100 boys and young men from the Winona Diocese. From the very beginning, enrollment numbers grew due to the quality of the education, extra-curricular activities, and beautiful setting.

As the effects of the Great Depression took hold, Saint Mary's achieved moderate growth in enrollment to 227 students in 1932. However, maintaining a college during the catastrophic economic times put financial strain on the Winona Diocese.

In 1933, the Brothers of the Christian Schools acquired the college from the Diocese of Winona, and a new trajectory for growth began. By 1942—thanks in large part to the network of Christian Brothers high schools—enrollment grew to 332.

The Second World War stifled enrollment growth as young men were called to serve their country. In an ironic twist, it was the United States Navy that might have saved Saint Mary's by locating an officers' training program on the Winona campus.

Like many colleges, Saint Mary's experienced robust growth thanks to the G.I. Bill and then the Baby Boom flooding American schools with eager students in an era of optimism. By 1962, enrollment was at 1,026 men.

The first year that women were admitted, a small number contributed to the overall enrollment of 977. But by 1972, women composed nearly one-quarter of the student body, and enrollment climbed to 1,135.

Graduate students began to make a significant impact on enrollment during the mid-1980s and combined enrollment rose to 1,683 students in 1987. Saint Mary's College became Saint Mary's University of Minnesota in 1994.

In the years that followed, undergraduate enrollment leveled off at a planned 1,300 students. Enrollment in graduate and professional programs continued to grow with new locations in Minnesota, Wisconsin, Nairobi (Kenya), and Jamaica, and with investments in facilities and programming.

Fueled by relevant and flexible programs for adult learners, the university serves a more diverse student body than ever before. During the 2012 centennial year, overall enrollment reached an all-time high of 5,919 students.

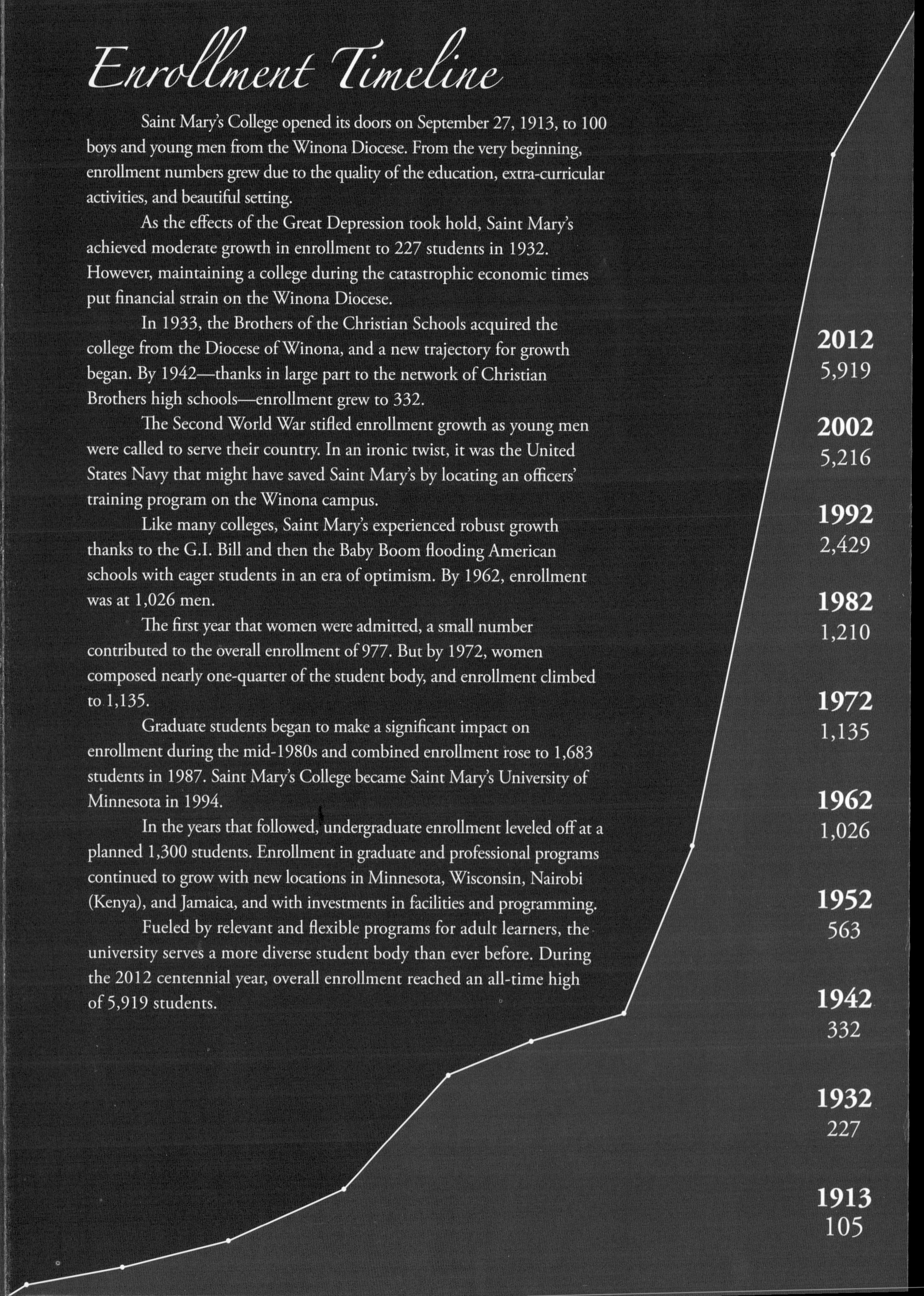

The U.S. Navy V-12 students, shown here in the summer of 1942, called themselves "Swabbies."

Carl Calabrese, a member of the 1942 basketball team, the only team to beat Hamline University the year it won the national small college championship.

In 1943, Brother Joel Nelson, president, and Brother Louis de La Salle, academic dean, followed a U.S. Navy officer during the review of the initial V-12 class at Saint Mary's College.

Brother H. Charles Severin, FSC

Brother H. Charles Severin, FSC, 1896–1992, professor of biology and eminent ecologist, received the title of Honorary President in 1985 from the college where he lived, taught, and inspired for nearly six decades. He modeled and encouraged throughout his life the qualities of teacher, scholar, and advisor that characterize the men and women who have educated students at Saint Mary's University of Minnesota during its first century.

Brother Charles was born in Bendena, Doniphan County, Kansas, on September 3, 1896, and graduated from Christian Brothers High School in St. Joseph, Missouri, in 1914. He entered the novitiate in Glencoe, Missouri, the following year.

While teaching at De la Salle Institute in Chicago, Brother Charles completed a B.S., an M.S., and a Ph.D. in Botany at the University of Chicago; his advisor was Dr. Henry Chandler Cowles, pioneering ecologist, botanist, teacher, and conservationist.

Brother Charles came to Saint Mary's College in 1933 with the first group of Brothers. He founded the Biology Department and with Dr. John Hoffman, head of the Chemistry Department, who began teaching at Saint Mary's in 1920, created an outstanding undergraduate science curriculum. Brother Charles also developed institutes, seminars, and summer courses to train high school teachers in laboratory and field techniques.

In addition to his course load and advising, Brother Charles directed the student health service and supervised the dispensary and infirmary on the second floor of Saint Mary's Hall. Students remember him as an expert, soothing presence in any emergency. One day, though, someone seeking help inquired, "Brother, what do you have for sunburn?" Brother Charles answered, "Contempt!"

From 1940 to 1965, Brother Charles edited *The American Biology Teacher*. In 1955, he was president of the National Association of Biology Teachers, which in 1963 honored him with its Distinguished Service Award. He wrote or co-wrote three biology textbooks and prepared an edition, on site, for the Republic of the Philippines. Brother Charles was elected Winona's "Man of the Year" in 1966.

Brother Charles taught Health and Hygiene at Saint Mary's after his retirement. The wing added to Hoffman Hall in 1988 is named in his honor. The Brother Charles Severin Award for Excellence in Teaching is an annual reminder of his impact on Saint Mary's University of Minnesota.

Brother Charles Severin was a well-known professor on the Winona campus, serving students and the community in many ways starting in 1933 up until his death in 1992.

Saint Mary's College undergrads enjoy Christmastime in 1943 with their neighbors at the College of Saint Teresa.

A 1943 photo of College of Saint Teresa students labeled, "The girls we dated."

The Saint Mary's College dance band at a mixer in 1943.

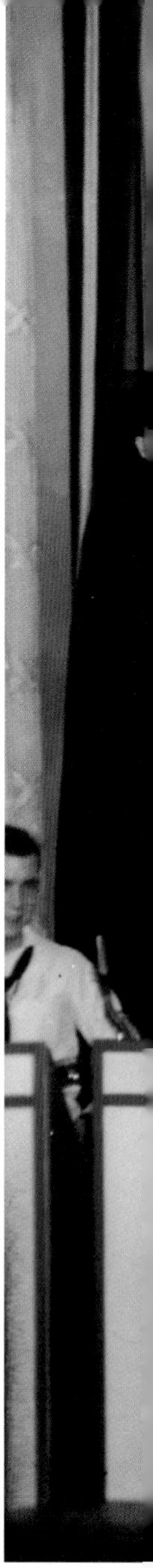

The 1943 edition of the annual "Redmen Revels" variety show.

The annual "Redmen Revels" in 1949 included a skit, "The Perils of Pauline."

Brother Joel Nelson, president; Brother Louis de La Salle, academic dean; and Navy officers saluted the flag during a review of the initial V-12 unit.

Saint Mary's produced Gilbert and Sullivan's The Mikado, *March 12–13, 1949.*

In the 1950s, Brother Paul Turner was credited with beginning the Phi Mu Alpha Sinfonia Chapter and the Candlelight Dinners as a way to raise money for music programs.

Brother Joachim Ambrose Groble, FSC
6th President, 1950–1956

Brother Joachim Ambrose Groble, FSC, the sixth president of Saint Mary's College, had a distinguished teaching and administrative career at Saint Mary's and, later, at Lewis University, Romeoville, Illinois.

A graduate of DePaul University in Chicago in the 1930s, when the Superior Scholasticate was located there, Brother Ambrose earned the M.S. in Education from the University of Minnesota. He joined the faculty at Saint Mary's College in 1941, a few months before the outbreak of World War II. He taught English and was chairman of the Education Department. In 1944, he became vice president of Saint Mary's College.

In 1950, the provincial of the St. Louis District appointed Brother Ambrose to succeed Brother Joel as president and director of the Brothers' community. During his presidency, he continued the expansion of campus facilities, including Aquinas (now Vlazny) Hall, a single-story student residence, and Hoffman Hall, the initial science wing of the future Adducci Science Center. He made faculty and curriculum development a priority and focused on obtaining government and private foundation grants. He authorized the graduate program with IBM, the M.Ed. summer program for Brothers, and the initiatives of the science faculty (Dr. John Hoffman, Brother Charles Severin, and Brother George Pahl, in particular) in providing summer graduate courses for secondary school teachers. He increased the college's success in gaining government-funded and privately sponsored programs. Undergraduate enrollment grew, slowly but steadily, from 542 to 780 during his term. Brother Ambrose returned to teaching at Saint Mary's in 1956.

In 1964, he transferred to the newly created Chicago District and taught Rhetoric and English at Lewis College (University), Romeoville, Illinois. An early environmentalist, Brother Ambrose shared his love of plants and trees with Brother Charles Severin at Saint Mary's and later planted hundreds of trees at Lewis University.

The Senior Class float in the 1950 Saint Mary's College homecoming parade in downtown Winona.

Students in the 1950s enjoyed all that college had to offer.

This 1950s aerial view shows, at left, St. Joseph Hall with added third floor and west wing; Rooney and Ditter Barracks, east of Heffron Hall; and to the west, Kelly Hall, the Immaculate Heart of Mary Seminary.

Pianist Jean Casadesus performs at Saint Mary's College in 1950. Brother Luke was the coordinator of the Community Concerts Series.

Speaking at the 1951 convocation, Brother Eliphus Victor, assistant to the superior general, honored Dr. Edward A. Fizpatrick, author of La Salle, Patron of All Teachers, *with a Doctor of Education degree. Seated are Brother Robert Shannon and Brother Martin Bertling.*

Guests at the dinner in honor of Dr. Edward A. Fitzpatrick in November 1951 were (left to right) Rt. Reverend Monsignor Bernard A. Kramer, Brother Victor, Dr. Fitzpatrick, and Brother Philip Matthews, provincial of the St. Louis District.

Brother Ignatius Basil Rothweiler, FSC

7th President, 1956–1963

Brother Ignatius Basil Rothweiler, FSC, the first alumnus (Class of 1938) to serve as president, was appointed the seventh president of Saint Mary's College in 1956. He was among the first group of Scholastics who earned their baccalaureate degree at Saint Mary's College.

Brother Basil arrived on campus in 1956 with an M.A. degree from St. Louis University and a wealth of experience as a secondary school teacher. He had previously served as dean of men at Saint Mary's College. As president, Brother Basil presided over a strong period of growth as the first postwar Baby Boomers began swelling the college's enrollment. He administered a successful capital campaign that funded the construction of two residence halls (St. Edward and Benilde), St. Thomas More Chapel, Fitzgerald Library, and La Salle Hall, a residence for the faculty Brothers, who since 1933 had been living in two-room apartments in Saint Mary's Hall and in student residence halls as advisors.

Bishop Edward Fitzgerald and Brother Basil were close friends and associates in support of the St. Yon Novitiate for the Brothers and the Immaculate Heart of Mary Seminary for the diocese. Brother Basil strengthened relationships with the Winona community and the Twin Cities business community during his presidency. The combined enrollment of the IHM Seminary, the St. Yon Novitiate, the St. Joseph Hall Scholasticate, and the new Damien Hall seminary of the Congregation of the Fathers of the Sacred Hearts of Jesus and Mary was between 150 and 200 students.

Brother Basil left Saint Mary's in 1963 to become the first provincial of the recently established Winona (later, St. Paul and Minneapolis) District. Saint Mary's College honored him with the degree of Doctor of Laws, *honoris causa,* on Founder's Day in 1978. In 2009, he celebrated his 75th year as a Christian Brother.

Art Smith (left) and Irwin Silchuk, co-captains of the 1951 football team.

The Marinotes entertain in the Union.

The 1952 homecoming bonfire on the Saint Mary's College campus.

Brother Ambrose Groble, president, broke ground for Aquinas Hall (now Vlazny Hall) in the spring of 1953.

Saint Mary's College won the 1953 MIAC baseball championship with an 11-1 record; Coach Max Molock is in row 3, far left.

Ed O'Malley, Saint Mary's football player, 1954.

Right-hander Walter Hill, a member of Max Molock's 1954 Saint Mary's College baseball team.

Brother Josephus Gregory Robertson, FSC
8th President, 1963–1969

Brother Josephus Gregory Robertson, FSC, a contemporary of Brother I. Basil Rothweiler, graduated from Saint Mary's College in 1939 with a B.S. in Mathematics. He earned an M.S. in Mathematics at Loyola University, Chicago, in 1942, and returned to Saint Mary's to teach Mathematics and Physics. From 1947 to 1952, he was Brother director of the Saint Mary's Scholasticate in St. Joseph Hall.

Brother Gregory left Saint Mary's in 1952 when the provincial of the St. Louis District appointed him director of novices in Glencoe, Missouri, and later in Winona at St. Yon Hall. In 1963, Brother Basil, the first provincial of the new Winona (St. Paul and Minneapolis) District, appointed Brother Gregory the eighth president of Saint Mary's College.

His six-year term was significant in many ways. He oversaw the construction of the new gymnasium in 1965; the conversion in 1966 of the old gymnasium as Skemp Hall, a three-story student residence named in honor of Coach Tom Skemp; and the building of the College Center (now the Michael H. Toner Student Center) in 1968. During his presidency, Saint Mary's introduced a modified calendar and an updated curriculum, became coeducational, and expanded the Board of Trustees by adding members in addition to the Brothers. The Psychology Department, independent study courses, and multidisciplinary courses were among the developments during his presidency.

Brother Gregory fostered cooperation with the College of Saint Teresa and with Winona State University. He was active in the fundraising and development projects sponsored by the Minnesota Private College Council.

Student Dennis O'Dwyer, Evanston, Illinois, poured coffee for a family during the 1954 Saint Mary's College Parents Weekend.

Winona Bishop Edward A. Fitzgerald presided at the 1954 dedication of Hoffman Hall, the science building, named in honor of a long-time professor, Dr. John J. Hoffman.

Brother Ambrose Groble (center) and Brother Philip Hogan, head of the Speech Department, chatted with Mr. and Mrs. John A. Gibney, Chicago, and sophomore John Gibney during Parents Weekend in 1956.

New students arrived on campus in 1956.

Max Molock gave a pep talk to his hockey players in the outdoor rink.

Brother I. Basil Rothweiler '38 (left) and Brother Julius Winkler '36 with Saint Mary's College honor students in 1961.

Benilde Hall, constructed in 1960, honors a French Brother beatified in 1958 and canonized in 1967.

Students prepared for homecoming in front of the barracks.

Damien Hall, on the west side of Highway 14 and since 1961 the seminary of the Congregation of the Sacred Hearts of Jesus and Mary, was purchased in 1972 by Saint Mary's College and renamed Watters Hall.

The original library in Saint Mary's Hall.

Cover of the 1960 fundraising brochure for the new Saint Mary's College library named in honor of Winona Bishop Edward Fitzgerald.

The men of Saint Mary's joined the women of the College of Saint Teresa for a traditional sock hop.

The Concert Chorus posed in the pine trees near Saint Mary's Park.

The Winona District of the Christian Brothers constructed St. Yon Hall in 1962 on the former Jahnke farm, across Gilmore Creek.

Winona's J. R. Watkins Co. offered the use of its airplane to fly the Saint Mary's College basketball team to a game with the University of Minnesota–Duluth in January 1961.

Archbishop Egidio Vagnozzi, apostolic delegate to the United States, in March 1962 blessed Leo Hall of Immaculate Heart of Mary Seminary. Monsignors George Speltz, rector, and William McGee accompanied him. Monsignor Roy Literski (at left) became the third rector of the seminary in 1968.

Of the 57 Saint Mary's College faculty in 1965, 37 percent were Brothers. Professor of philosophy Father Andrew Fabian, OP, at left in the fourth row, is still teaching at Saint Mary's University.

The outdoor ice rink was the scene of a game between Saint Mary's College and Saint John's, Collegeville, in the winter of 1963.

At the Saint Mary's College 1964 Founder's Day convocation were (left to right) Dr. William Blass, Physics; Brother Robert Lane, History; Brother Julius Winkler, academic dean; Brother J. Gregory Robertson, president; Monsignor William E. McManus, Chicago, the honoree, future Bishop of Fort Wayne-South Bend, Indiana; and Bishop Edward Fitzgerald of Winona.

In 1964, the entrance road to Saint Mary's College ran between Hoffman Hall and St. Thomas More Chapel to Highway 14.

In 1965, the Minnesota Highway Department constructed a pedestrian bridge over Highway 14 near Hoffman Hall.

In the 1960s, high school science teachers took summer graduate courses in Winona that were funded by the National Science Foundation; the photographer was most likely Brother Charles Severin, the program director.

Seven of the Brothers who were at Saint Mary's College in 1966 were (left to right) Brother Joseph de La Salle, Brother Anthony Sullivan, Brother Francis Walsh, Brother Gregory Robertson, president, Brother Edward Chism, Brother Patrick Hayes, and Brother Justus Morneau.

Brother Leonard Courtney (left) and Brother George Pahl (right) visited with Joan and Carl Calabrese '41 at a Twin Cities Saint Mary's College alumni event in 1968.

Coach Ken Wiltgen, Cody Hanzel, and Brother Gregory Robertson, president, at a 1968 Saint Mary's College event in the Twin Cities.

In the fall of 1968, the last freshman class entered when Saint Mary's College was a men's college.

Chapter 3

COEDUCATION: 1969–1983

The peace and social justice movements that inspired debates and demonstrations at Saint Mary's College during the 1960s and 1970s accented another significant development. In 1969, after more than half a century as an all-male institution, Saint Mary's College admitted women as full-time, undergraduate, resident students.

Inspired and invited by Vatican Council II (1962–1965), religious orders re-examined their mission and their Rule in light of their founding charism and contemporary needs. The De La Salle Christian Brothers, by Rule and custom, did not teach girls, but their General Chapter of 1966–1967 promulgated and received Vatican approval of the revised Rule and Constitutions, which encouraged the association of dedicated men and women in the educational work of the Institute in schools at every level for boys and girls.

As enrollment at Saint Mary's College reached a plateau of 1,000 students in the 1960s, after increasing nearly 60 percent between 1955 and 1961, the idea grew that coeducation might be a necessary step.

Moreover, vocations to the Brothers were declining in number. The high point in their worldwide membership, 16,824 Brothers with vows, occurred in 1965. By the late 1960s, the Winona Scholasticate was experiencing a significant downward trend from the years when one hundred or more Brother Scholastics were on campus annually.

Freshman Tony Piscitiello arrived at Saint Mary's College in 1965 after graduating from St. Mel High School in Chicago. His role model was Brother Patrick Hayes, vice president of development, and when Tony graduated in 1969, his first job was admissions counselor under Brother Anthony Sullivan's direction.

Saint Mary's College was dealing with a troubling enrollment decline. The freshman class dropped from 310 in 1967 to 243 in 1968, and then to 236 in 1969. In that year, the enrollment fell below 1,000 for the first time

The face of Saint Mary's changed in 1969 as the college became co-educational. Both men and women benefited from the strength of the science programs.

Aquinas Hall residents worked on their entry in the 1970 Winter Sports Weekend snow sculpture competition.

In 1973, the Environmental Awareness Program offered a physical education course in Winter Camping.

since 1964 and was the lowest enrollment at Saint Mary's College since 1960.

The decision to admit women as full-time undergraduates did not surprise students, faculty, and administrators, but the change certainly took some time to settle in and to become routine.

Many of the initial women students at Saint Mary's College already were connected through a father, uncle, brother, or friend who had attended the college. Tony Piscitiello recalled meeting with one Chicago family during their visit on campus in 1969. The father, a Saint Mary's graduate, and the mother, a graduate of Saint Teresa, stated that if their daughter was going to be a biologist, she was going to attend Saint Mary's.

There was more interest and receptivity among young women from Winona, Rochester, and southeastern Minnesota communities than from the Twin Cities area. Because of the longstanding pipeline to Chicago, Saint Mary's College enrolled a number of young women from Chicago in 1969 and in the 1970s, including some who transferred from junior and community colleges.

The women in those first years shared a natural camaraderie because of their unique situation. A few of the new faculty members were younger than some students who were veterans of military service or were completing their bachelor's degree.

The opening of the College Center (now the Michael H. Toner Student Center) in 1969 was critical to the smooth integration of women students. The Center's new dining hall replaced the cramped facilities in Griffin Hall. Students involved in the Student Senate and many clubs and activities had a new building to call their own. Practical matters needed attention, too, such as the availability of hair dryers in residence halls (although a trend toward long hair for men made that issue moot for most of the 1970s).

More serious questions came to the fore, according to Dr. Marilyn Frost, none more important than whether Saint Mary's was a coeducational college or a men's college that allows women to attend and graduate. Because few Brothers had ever taught women in their classes, the 1970s were years of adjustment. "The Brothers had to change their way of teaching to accommodate women," Dr. Larry Luttmers said. "With women in the classroom, a lot of their assumptions and stereotypes were proved wrong."

By the mid-1970s, women comprised more than a quarter of the Saint Mary's College enrollment. They participated in the classroom and became an integral part of campus life. Graduates from those days talk fondly of memories of the Mole Hole, the Center, the Pub, Steak Night, food fights, meal cards, and pledging. They enjoyed Winter Sports Weekend and played flag football

A typical room in a Saint Mary's College residence hall in 1975.

Graffiti from each theatre production decorated the walls backstage of the then third-floor theatre in Saint Mary's Hall.

on the fields below the bluffs. They went on dates to Shorty's, Roy's Roadhouse, Walt's, and the Golden Frog across the river in Fountain City, and the Oaks in Minnesota City. They joined their sisters for pizza at Shakey's and Rocco's.

The coeducation decision helped stem the enrollment erosion at Saint Mary's College. Slightly more than 1,200 students enrolled in 1977, and the total remained above 1,200 for the next six years. For the first time, Saint Mary's College in 1981 enrolled more than 400 freshmen. The 1970s and 1980s also were years when the student population gradually shifted from 60 percent of Chicagoland origin to 75 percent from Minnesota.

In 2003, Saint Mary's College established the Saint Teresa Leadership and Service Institute to foster, within an academic setting, a spiritual, social, and cultural environment through which the leadership potential of women is nurtured. Students in the Institute live in a shared community on campus and participate in a living and learning co-curricular program. The women gain many of the benefits of an all-women's education within the coeducational Saint Mary's community. Select general education courses are offered in women-focused classes, and the students in the institute complete a course series in leadership and service. Approximately 20 freshman and sophomore women are admitted to the Saint Teresa Institute at the beginning of each fall semester.

The admission of women to Saint Mary's College was not the only notable change during the period. Between 1968 and 1974, Saint Mary's College, with the support of the district administration of the Brothers, established an independent Board of Trustees, with all the members, except the president, coming from outside the college, including the Brothers on the board. The new Board of Trustees formalized the separation of the administration of Saint Mary's College from that of the Brothers' district. As a result, the faculty and the student body governance also changed.

The admission of women transformed Saint Mary's and set the stage for a major change in the 1990s, from college to university. The transformation begun in 1969 was so noncontroversial and organic (including the recruitment of women to the faculty and staff) as to be rarely noted 40-some years later. The adaptation was a practical one, preserving the personal and helping atmosphere on campus and meeting situations and problems with common sense as they arose. One veteran faculty member said that she would guess a lot of women students today do not even know that Saint Mary's was once a men's college.

Women had settled onto campus by the time Brother Peter Clifford was named president in 1976.

During his tenure, Brother Peter set the stage for growth and prosperity, putting the university's finances back in the black. He initiated the first graduate course offerings in the Twin Cities and laid the financial groundwork for the Performance Center and the ice arena. A proponent of community involvement, Brother Peter retired in 1984. He returned to Saint Mary's to work with the Metanoia Group from 2000 to 2002.

Brother George Pahl, president, at left, visited with guests at a Saint Mary's College Alumni Christmas Dance in Chicago in 1971.

This 1969 photo illustrates two changes on the Saint Mary's College campus: the demise of the old Union and the addition of cars on campus.

Homecoming in 1970 was a trip down memory lane.

In 1970, younger alumni at homecoming enjoyed a volleyball game.

The May 1971 graduation displayed a variety of styles during a decade of change.

Saint Mary's College students attended a 1971 Student Senate meeting in the Hall of Fame Room.

Coach Max Molock and his players searched for Marc Weisenburger's contact lens during a 1972 game.

Dr. Donald Morgan, Physics Department, at left, and Brother George Pahl, president, at right, visited with Minnesota Congressman Al Quie during his visit to Saint Mary's in 1972.

Phi Gamma Mu members encouraged a new student in the Ek Family Student Village to pledge in 1973.

Women in dormitories in 1973.

Fraternities and sororities were popular on campus in the '60s, '70s, and '80s. Pictured here is the Alpha Kappa Psi fraternity in 1974.

Brother George Pahl, FSC

9th President, 1969–1976

Brother George Pahl, FSC, a 1936 graduate of Saint Mary's College, was appointed the ninth president of Saint Mary's College in 1969. He earned an M.S. in Biology at DePaul University, Chicago, and a Ph.D. in Radiation Biology at the University of Notre Dame.

A native of Minneapolis, Brother George taught high school biology at De La Salle Institute in Chicago from 1936 to 1942, when the provincial of the St. Louis District assigned him to teach Biology at Saint Mary's College. Brother George was renowned for research and teaching in the field of radiation oncology. With Brother Charles Severin, he pioneered summer teacher training programs supported by the National Science Foundation.

Highlights of Brother George's presidency are the reorganization of the Board of Trustees in 1970, the purchase of Damien Hall from the Congregation of the Sacred Hearts of Jesus and Mary in 1972, the purchase of St. Joseph Hall and the leasing of St. Yon Hall in 1974 from the Brothers' District, and the construction of two student apartment villages, Ek Family Village in 1971 and Village II in 1973.

Curriculum changes during Brother George's presidency include the creation of the Fine Arts Department, a new Sociology major, and a psychology laboratory; revision of the general education program; and introduction of independent study, individualized major, allied health care, computer science, and human development programs.

Brother George reorganized the administration into four major areas, each headed by a vice president: academic affairs, student development, financial affairs, and college relations. He developed a broader base of income for Saint Mary's, including the $1.5-million Advanced Institutional Development Program grant in 1975 from the U.S. Department of Education.

At the end of his term as president, Brother George received the Bishop Heffron Award in recognition of his contribution to the development of Saint Mary's College.

With Larry Gilhooly as manager and Jerry Sauer (top right) as chef, Saint Mary's College ran its own food service. Students from the 1970s and 1980s remember steak nights, work/study jobs (like Ted Vatch's, at right), and the friendly staff.

Intramural sports played an important role in campus life.

One 1975 freshman pondered what was next on the schedule (left); another, in 1976, perhaps wondered how the family back home was doing (right).

Brother Peter Clifford, FSC

10th President, 1976–1984

Brother Peter Clifford, FSC, the 10th president of Saint Mary's College and the first Brother selected by the Board of Trustees after a nationwide search in all districts, is a native of New York City. He earned a B.A. at Manhattan College in 1951, an M.A. at Fordham University in 1957, and an Ed.D. at Harvard University in 1970. He did additional study at the University of Santo Tomas in Manila, Republic of the Philippines, and at New York University's Graduate School of Business.

Brother Peter's career in the Long Island-New England District prior to his presidency at Saint Mary's College consisted of teaching and educational administration on the East Coast in Catholic elementary and secondary schools in New York City and at Saint John's University, Jamaica, New York, where he was associate dean of the School of Education.

His tenure at Saint Mary's College encompassed a period of institutional growth and of faculty and curriculum development in the context of the declining number of vocations to the Christian Brothers. He improved the college's planning and budgeting processes and achieved an annual operating balance, after overcoming a $250,000 deficit in the current fund. He left for his successor a $3-million overall current and endowment fund balance. Brother Peter authorized the college's initial graduate course offerings in the Twin Cities and laid the financial groundwork for the construction of the Performance Center (Page Theatre and Figliulo Recital Hall) and the ice arena.

Brother Peter forged a close working relationship with the Winona community. He served on the boards of the Winona Chamber of Commerce and Norwest Bank. In 1982–1984, he was the president of the Minnesota Private College Council. He was a board member of Christian Brothers Investment Services, Inc., and of Ocean Tides, a Lasallian residential and educational facility in Narragansett, Rhode Island.

Viewing the 1976 Founder's Day honorary degree citation were (left to right) Brother Luke Herbert; Brother Gabriel Moran, the honoree, of the Long Island-New England District; Brother George Pahl, president; Brother Julius Winkler; and Dr. Richard Jarvinen.

The Saint Mary's College Madrigal Singers performed in 1976.

Robert Connor was one of many Saint Mary's College faculty members who traveled to Chicago to advise prospective students in 1978.

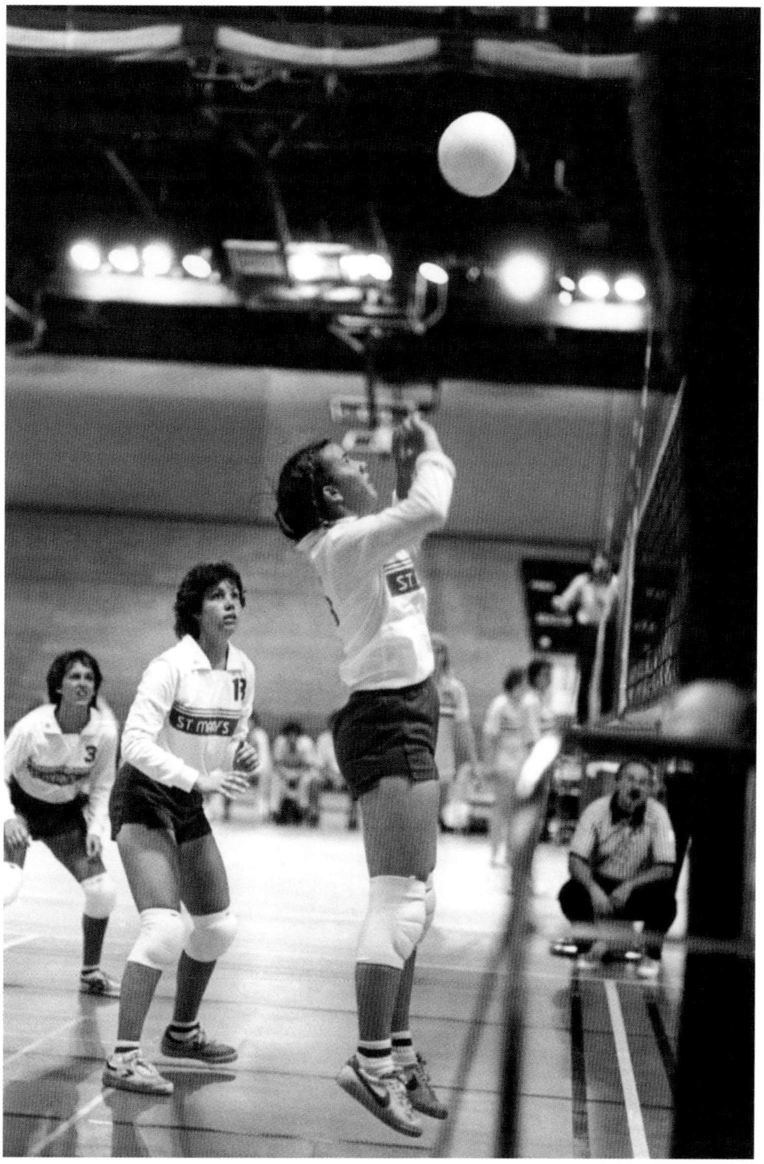

Saint Mary's College volleyball players in 1981.

Saint Mary's hockey played in "the bubble"—an air-supported dome—for several years until a new arena was completed in 1987.

George Stephenson (right), Class of 1980, 2000 Hall of Fame honoree, was a four-year letter-winner and three-year team captain. He became the first and only individual Saint Mary's College national champion by winning the 1978 National Catholic Championships at Notre Dame University. His career record of 85-28-1 ranked him number one in Saint Mary's history.

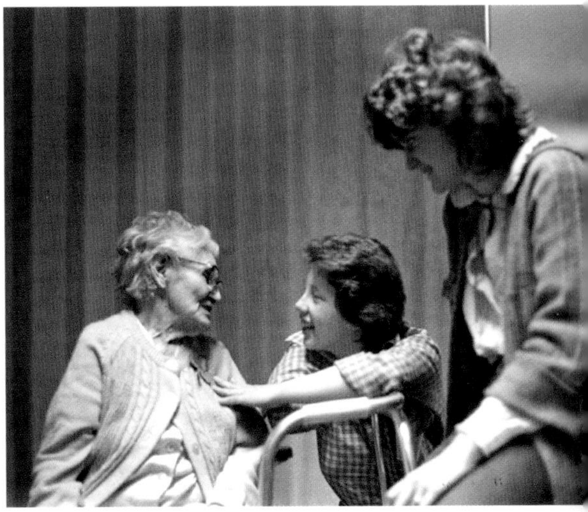

Students volunteered in 1979 for Big Brothers-Big Sisters and Foster Grandparents.

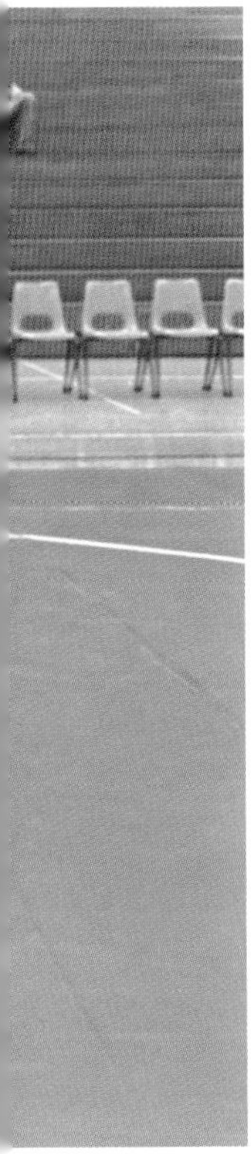

Saint Mary's College student Kathy Burns consulted with financial aid officer Pat Hubbard in 1980.

More than 500 people attended the June 1979 ceremony in which Saint Mary's honored Dr. Joseph Kraft '43, chairman of Clinical Pathology and Nuclear Medicine at St. Joseph's Hospital, Chicago, with the Distinguished Alumnus Award. Pictured (left to right) are Dr. Bill Rock '49, a previous recipient; Brian Kraft; Mrs. Joseph Kraft; Dr. Joseph Kraft; his mother, Mrs. Ella Kraft (seated); Bishop George Speltz, St. Cloud; and Lloyd Kraft.

athy Faul during the 1978 Winter Sports Weekend.

This 1970s aerial view shows the spread of Saint Mary's College facilities across the open field of the 1920s.

An iconic entrance sign now graces the road to St. Yon Hall.

Winter Sports Weekend in the late 1970s and early 1980s featured touch football, broomball (above), and sledding (left).

Students engaged in classroom discussion in late 1970s.

Mona Frana found a quiet place to study in 1980.

Graduates celebrated after the ceremony in 1980.

Chapter 4

EXPANSION: 1984–2012

Two name changes by Saint Mary's College in the 1990s serve as a prelude to this chapter. In 1990, Saint Mary's College changed its name to Saint Mary's College of Minnesota to distinguish itself from other colleges in the U.S. with the Saint Mary's name. The name change to Saint Mary's University of Minnesota, on October 20, 1994, resulted from achieving accreditation as a university from the Higher Learning Commission of the North Central Association of Colleges and Schools.

Years of preparation and curriculum development at undergraduate and graduate levels preceded this renewed and upgraded accreditation. The university accreditation and name change occurred at the midpoint of the 21-year presidency of Brother Louis DeThomasis, but his intent from the start of his presidency was to transform a college into a university.

Global Initiatives

Although it might be tempting to stereotype the growth of Saint Mary's University of Minnesota during these 21 years as merely that of a vibrant, urban, graduate campus in the Twin Cities metro area combined with a traditional, residential, liberal arts, undergraduate campus in Winona, nothing could be farther from the truth.

When Brother Louis became its 11th president in 1984, he set about reaffirming the Lasallian charism and tradition at Saint Mary's College and providing new traction to three centuries of Lasallian history of service to people most in need of education. He intended to globalize Saint Mary's College to a point where it would no longer be just a small, traditional college.

His globalization strategy stemmed from his years of study at Georgetown University's School of Foreign Service. In Winona, he created the De La Salle Language Institute and placed it under the leadership of Dr. Daniel Maloney. He launched the recruitment of international students, initially from Mexico and Central America. His initiatives helped to create an international campus in Winona. He encouraged initiatives in China

Brother Louis DeThomasis arrived in Winona as Saint Mary's 11th president.

Brother William Mann was inaugurated as the 13th president of Saint Mary's University in 2008.

In 1984, Saint Mary's College played the College of St. Thomas in the Hubert H. Humphrey Metrodome in Minneapolis.

and in Taiwan, long before China's economic prowess became the leading international story. Brother Louis traveled to China to help recruit international students.

During the 1980s, the undergraduate campus in Winona developed international programs in Florence, Italy, and in London, England. Dr. Michael Flanagan, a Chicago native and a graduate of St. Mel High School and Saint Mary's College, returned to teach at Saint Mary's in 1967. In 1993, while on sabbatical in London, he scouted locations for the Saint Mary's Theatre Department junior year abroad program. Undergraduate theatre majors spend a semester of their junior year in London and study and attend productions at venues such as the Globe Theatre and the Old Vic. The first students went to London in 1994. This became known as the Stefannié Valéncia Kierlin London Theatre Program. Today, 12 to 20 juniors go each year, and new students enroll in the theatre program because of the experience.

For Brother Louis, these steps were not enough. He helped establish the Christ the Teacher Institute for Education (CTIE), one of seven institutes of higher learning that comprise Tangaza College in Nairobi, Kenya. Founded in 1992, CTIE is affiliated with Saint Mary's University, which awards the bachelor's degree to students who complete the four-year academic program. Originally founded to educate members of religious communities, CTIE prepares an increasing number of laypeople from Kenya and other African countries to teach in secondary schools. CTIE offers two undergraduate programs in education; the associated Maryknoll Institute of African Studies offers two graduate programs. Veteran Saint Mary's professor Brother Leonard Courtney assisted Brother Louis in the process of evaluating and accrediting CTIE.

Brother Louis also established a relationship with the Catholic College of Mandeville in Jamaica in which Saint Mary's University offers a graduate program in education with the Jamaican institution.

Saint Mary's College and Abbott Northwestern Hospital formed the Graduate Institute and offered courses in 1984 in leased space at 2500 Park Avenue South, Minneapolis.

Growth and Expansion in Winona

The Winona campus expanded with Brother Louis at the helm. In addition to a new ice arena and the Performance Center, new construction in the late 1980s included Brother Charles Hall, an addition to Hoffman Hall, in 1987 (the two form the Adducci Science Center), the Christian Brothers' residence in 1988, and the Gilmore Creek student residence in 1989. Saint Thomas More Chapel, the facilities of the Art Department and the Music Department, and most classrooms and residence halls underwent extensive renovation in the late 1980s and early 1990s.

The Winona campus' construction boom continued after 1990. The Recreation and Athletic Center (RAC), including Gostomski Fieldhouse and Jul Gernes Pool, and the McEnery Center addition to Fitzgerald Library opened in 1994, followed by the Pines student residence in 1995, the Hendrickson

Center addition to Saint Mary's Hall in 1996, the Heights academic building in 1997, the Hillside student residence in 2001, and the track and field complex and Leo Ochrymowycz Memorial Soccer Field in 2009. Hoffman Hall underwent interior renovation funded by the National Science Foundation.

Saint Mary's University revamped the core curriculum and reorganized the academic administration into four schools: Arts, Business, Education, and Humanities and Sciences. One example of the innovative curriculum on the Winona campus is the Nuclear Medicine Technology Program, which has placed graduates at every Mayo Clinic facility in the United States.

Saint Mary's University received national recognition for a number of its Winona programs and acclaim for its Tegrity Lecture Capture technology, one of the first of its kind in the nation. The science, computer science, theatre, and college-bound programs attracted hundreds of students annually. Bush Foundation grant programs hosted by Saint Mary's University have been noteworthy across the region.

The faculty and staff in Winona developed Lilly Foundation grants, the Path to Academic Success (PASS) Program, and the Lasallian Honors Program. Faculty and students won federal and state grants and national renown for their environmental monitoring of the Mississippi River below the Prairie Island Nuclear Plant.

Dr. Jeffrey Highland joined the faculty in 1977 as a political scientist. After teaching for a decade, he accepted increasingly important administrative roles under Brother Louis. From 2000 until his retirement in 2009, Dr. Highland was university provost and vice president of the college. As chief academic officer, he worked to strengthen the general education curriculum of the college, to support the development of new graduate and professional programs, and to oversee the successful reaccreditation process ending in 2006.

Over his 32-year tenure, Dr. Highland saw Saint Mary's become bigger and more complex. "Our mission pushed us to expand our range of service to students. We went from primarily a liberal arts college to a doctoral-granting institution with multiple campuses, centers, and sites."

A popular and visible figure on the Winona campus, Dr. Highland was master of ceremonies at major university events, a piano accompanist, and a mentor to the Phi Mu Alpha music fraternity. In 1988, Dr. Highland was honored by the Christian Brothers as a Distinguished Lasallian Educator, and in 2002, the order named him an Affiliate Member.

Dr. Jeffrey Highland, a popular and visible teacher and administrator during his 32-year career.

Go Cardinals!

The ongoing transformation of undergraduate and graduate programs did not mean that longstanding traditions disappeared. Cardinal athletic teams flourished on the undergraduate campus in Winona and enjoyed three new facilities: the ice arena, the Recreation and Athletic Center, and the track and soccer complex.

Saint Mary's University of Minnesota once belonged to the National Association of Intercollegiate Athletics (NAIA), but since the early 1980s has competed in varsity intercollegiate sports as a member of the National Collegiate Athletic Association (NCAA), Division III. The addition of women's hockey in 1998 raised to 21 the number of intercollegiate sports at the university. Broad-based participation is the rule, in keeping with Division III's objectives. Student athletes enjoy a range of opportunities to integrate athletics and academic excellence.

Donny Nadeau '85, former sports journalist and current sports information director, jumped at the opportunity to return to Saint Mary's University. Several

Dr. William Ammentorp, advisor to Brother Peter Clifford and to Brother Louis DeThomasis, applied computer technology in his 1983 course at the Minneapolis Graduate Center.

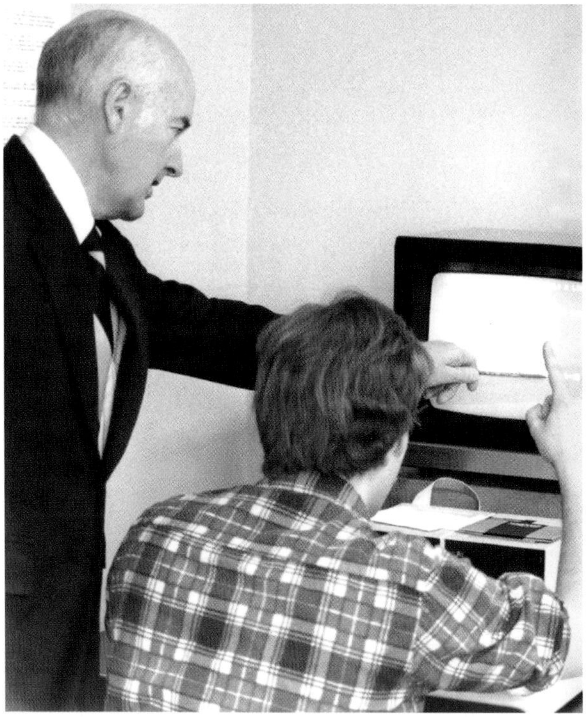

other staff members are graduates of Saint Mary's; they agree that their experiences during their undergraduate years were special and long-lasting. Nadeau noted that people might not realize what good students the athletes must be to participate in Division III athletics. Saint Mary's student athletes include All-Americans and some of the university's brightest students.

Athletic Director Nicole Fennern pointed out that in 2010, student athletes were the valedictorian and the salutatorian of the graduating class. In recent years, several student athletes have been the university's male and female outstanding seniors. Student athletes can practice 20 to 30 hours a week and still are able to succeed academically and in all other areas of campus life. They cherish for a lifetime the relationships and the experiences of being a member of an athletic team.

The most exciting recent event in Cardinal athletics was the victory of the Saint Mary's University fastpitch softball team in the 2000 NCAA Division III national championship competition. Although the Cardinals finished second to the University of St. Thomas in the Minnesota Intercollegiate Athletic Conference (MIAC) standings, their 33-6 record earned them an at-large berth in the tournament. They won seven consecutive post-season games in pursuit of the first national title ever won by a Saint Mary's team. John Tschida '90, an outstanding baseball shortstop, coached the women's team to a record 40 wins en route to the national title. The Cardinals won the 2000 NCAA Division III national championship in Salem, Virginia, by defeating Ithaca College and the College of New Jersey and then winning two games against Chapman University with the final victory, 5-0, on May 19, 2000. The season had begun with 369 teams nationwide playing NCAA Division III fastpitch softball. In 2005, the 2000 national championship team was inducted into in the Saint Mary's University of Minnesota Sports Hall of Fame.

The Cardinals placed five players on the national all-tournament team: Jill Hocking (also named an All-American), Jackie Huegel, Jennifer Miller, Laura Miller, and Jennifer Meyer. Jennifer Miller returned to Saint Mary's University in 2007 and is currently the head coach of the Cardinals fastpitch team. Jill Hocking earned All-American honors and was also a top-30 finalist for the NCAA Woman of the Year Award, a considerable honor because it combines athletes from all three NCAA divisions.

By the dawn of the 21st century, 22 to 25 percent of Saint Mary's University undergraduates were competing in intercollegiate athletics. Amanda Weinmann, the first Saint Mary's University post-graduate NCAA recipient, was a three-time All-American in track and field, and in 2007 she was also a top-30 finalist across all three divisions for the NCAA Woman of the Year Award.

An award of special meaning and significance to the Saint Mary's University of Minnesota athletic program was in recognition of community service in the local flood relief of August 2007. The NCAA Division III awarded the NCAA/Jostens Community Service Project Award, with $1,000 of general scholarship funds, to Saint Mary's University athletes for their efforts in aiding flood victims in the Winona area during the devastating floods of 2007. Nearly 200 athletes and coaches representing 10 sports volunteered to sort clothing, deliver food and water, clear debris, and repair homes. As Brother William Mann, the president, said, "Adversity brings out goodness in people. In this case, our student athletes recognized the opportunity they had as individuals, and more powerfully as teams, to share their strong hearts, minds, and bodies to make a difference in putting lives back together. Many members of our own Saint Mary's family lost everything in the August 2007 flood, and this was a reminder that we have the opportunity to serve each other right here in this campus community."

Intramural teams and competitions have also been a continuing major activity at Saint Mary's University over the years. Few students pass through the university without some exposure to intramurals, whether indoor or outdoor. Recreational activities are also encouraged and supported. Thanks to the decades-long work of Brother Jerome Rademacher and others, the Winona campus boasts one of the finest networks of cross-country ski trails in the Midwest. Saint Mary's campus in Winona is an outstanding, inspiring environment. The Environmental Awareness Program encourages students to hike, to camp (with Brother Finbar McMullen in winter), to canoe (with Brother John Grover), and to play disc golf.

Graduate Programs

The graduate programs of Saint Mary's University transformed a Catholic liberal arts college in Winona, Minnesota, into a growing university that now provides graduate education to a large cross-section of Minnesotans. On the undergraduate residential campus in Winona, at the adult learning complex south of downtown Minneapolis, and in satellite facilities in the Twin Cities metro area, Rochester, and more than 100 school districts in Minnesota and western Wisconsin, Saint Mary's University of Minnesota offers graduate and professional programs in a host of subject areas, including education, business, counseling and psychological services, and advanced practice nursing.

The graduate program traces its roots to the decision by IBM to build a major manufacturing plant in Rochester, Minnesota, in the 1950s. At the time, Saint Mary's College already had a reputation for excellence in teaching and learning. At its 50th anniversary point, in 1962–63, the Saint Mary's College faculty included 30 with doctorates, or 45 percent of the total. In the early 1960s, more than 60 percent of Saint Mary's College graduates continued their education in graduate or professional schools.

Saint Mary's College received significant grants from federal education funding in the 1950s and 1960s to support graduate courses on the Terrace Heights campus. For example, Dr. Leo Ochrymowycz taught Scientific German to Mayo Clinic personnel who drove to Winona from Rochester. Brother Charles Severin taught graduate courses in environmental biology long before something called the environmental movement came into being.

When IBM approached Brother Basil Rothweiler, the president, in October 1960 about providing graduate courses at its Rochester complex, Saint Mary's quickly responded. IBM had built a plant to manufacture IBM keypunch-reader computers. When

Saint Mary's College played a home game against Augsburg College in 1986.

Saint Mary's College began offering graduate courses on the IBM campus in 1961, Big Blue was employing more than 2,300 people at its Rochester site.

The agreement with IBM called for Saint Mary's College to provide the faculty for a graduate study program for selected employees. Successful completion of these courses led to a master's degree in physics and mathematics. Saint Mary's established a top-level technological relationship with IBM that resulted in the installation in the mid-1960s on the Winona campus of an IBM 1130 to handle data processing tasks.

In the 1970s and through the mid-1980s, Saint Mary's College offered a number of graduate courses on the Winona campus. During the last two years of Brother Peter Clifford's presidency, 1983 and 1984, Saint Mary's began offering a limited number of graduate courses in St. Paul, in rented space at Cretin High School, and at Saint John's Hospital to help adult learners work toward a master's degree in human development and psychology.

In the 1980s, faculty on the Winona campus were developing graduate programs that Saint Mary's College, during the presidency of Brother Louis, would offer in the Twin Cities. The Master of Education, the largest graduate program in the 1980s, began on the Winona campus. The Master of Arts in Instruction (MAI) and the GeoSpatial Services (GSS) program also started in Winona and later expanded to the Minneapolis campus. GSS also added a component to undertake professional consulting work. The master's degree in philanthropy and development also originated on the Winona campus.

During the final two decades of the 20th century, the undergraduate faculty of Saint Mary's

In the 1980s, Saint Mary's College added men's and women's soccer to the intercollegiate athletic program. The 1986 women's soccer team led by Coach Dan Blank was one of several that appeared in national tournaments and earned All-American honors in the late 1980s and early 1990s.

University developed or assisted with other graduate programs, such as the Master of Arts in International Business (MIB) and the Professional Development Initiatives for Educators (PDI). They worked with special diligence to develop the K-12 Reading Licensure Program and the Special Education Program, two of the largest graduate offerings by Saint Mary's University. By the early 1990s, 30 percent of the revenue of the Schools of Graduate and Professional Programs came from Winona-based programs.

By the early 1980s, undergraduate enrollment in Winona plateaued around 1,250 students; a record 1,272 students registered for the 1980–81 academic year. Before that year ended, however, Minnesota found itself mired in a national recession, the worst economic downturn since the Great Depression. The restructuring of the U.S. steel industry meant massive layoffs on Minnesota's Iron Range. Crop prices plummeted after President Jimmy Carter's embargo of the Soviet Union because of its 1979 occupation of Afghanistan. Minnesota farm exports fell dramatically, and farmland in the state significantly declined in price through the mid-1980s. These economic upheavals led to declining enrollment. With 1,193 students in fall 1983, Saint Mary's found itself, for the first time since 1976, with fewer than 1,200 students. The total remained below 1,200 until the fall of 1988.

Bishop Loras Watters, the fifth Bishop of Winona, walked in a campus procession in 1989. Saint Mary's College renamed Damien Hall as Watters Hall in his honor.

Brother Louis DeThomasis

In 1984, the Saint Mary's Board of Trustees appointed Brother Louis DeThomasis the 11th president of Saint Mary's College. He came to Winona on a mission to change the college's culture. Faculty and staff were dealing with the challenges of enrollment and of designing a curriculum to meet current needs. Job losses in Minnesota during the 1981–1983 recession were severe. Thousands of Minnesotans were seeking an opportunity to retrain, to cross-train, or to better themselves with a college degree.

Brother Louis was in a unique position with a unique set of talents and experiences to ensure that Saint Mary's served Minnesota citizens in these economic circumstances. As a high school senior at La Salle Military Academy, Long Island, he had wanted to be a Brother. "I visited the novitiate, but my parents thought that I was too young. Those were the days when you listened to your parents." Instead, Brother Louis enrolled at Georgetown University, Washington, D.C., in the fall of 1958. After earning a bachelor's degree from Georgetown's School of Foreign Service, he studied for a year at the University of Madrid. Returning to the United States in 1964, he still had the Brother's vocation in mind, but first he started a printing shop in Washington, D.C., and became a successful young business leader. Because his shop was at the forefront of the offset printing revolution, his prices were competitive, and he secured a government contract to print U.S. patents. His business expanded into the Maryland suburbs, and he invested in a start-up Maryland bank.

At the age of 26, Brother Louis passed the printing business to his brother and then completed the novitiate of the Long Island-New England District. Because of his business experience, the district assigned him to administrative positions. "I came into Catholic education in the early 1970s as things were crumbling," Brother Louis explained. "I only taught full-time for two years. I spent the next eight years in administration. In 1981, I started Christian Brothers Investment Services, Inc., which now has $4 billion under investment management for Catholic dioceses, schools, hospitals, and organizations."

Speaking of his initial view of Saint Mary's College, Brother Louis said, "It was a wonderful Catholic residential college and needed a new approach." He reasoned that expanding the undergraduate college

In 1988, Brother Louis DeThomasis, president (right), hosted Joseph Cardinal Bernardin, Cardinal-Archbishop of Chicago, on the Winona campus.

was not structurally wise and that increasing the entire graduate program in Winona made no sense either.

Saint Mary's was already a pioneer, since the 1950s, in bringing graduate education to adult leaders in a non-traditional way. "As a result," Brother Louis said, Saint Mary's "took a lot of flak in the beginning with our Lasallian approach. We were on the forefront of developing quality programs in a non-traditional way."

Partnership with Abbott Northwestern Hospital

Saint Mary's established a graduate partnership program in Minneapolis in 1983, one year before Brother Louis began his presidency. Abbott Northwestern Hospital asked Saint Mary's to help set up a graduate program to educate students for nurse anesthesia work at the hospital. Abbott Northwestern officials told Saint Mary's officials that they had long been impressed with the student-centered vision and commitment to social responsibility of Saint Mary's. The two institutions quickly partnered on a joint venture program that used the facilities of Abbott Northwestern Hospital and the faculty of Saint Mary's College. James McCovey, then the president of Abbott Northwestern Hospital, was a key figure in moving the joint venture forward, and Gordon Springer, of his staff, a Minneapolis De La Salle High School graduate, worked closely with Saint Mary's officials on the graduate school partnership.

Merri Moody, future dean of the Saint Mary's Graduate School of Health and Human Services, did her nursing training at St. Mary of Nazareth Hospital in Chicago in the 1970s and worked as an Intensive Care Unit nurse for seven years in the Chicago area. She wanted to further her education with a nurse anesthesia program, and Abbott Northwestern Hospital's program with Saint Mary's was a perfect fit. Moody, as a student, saw a different perspective at the time. Abbott Northwestern Hospital owned the program, a small one with only 10 students per class, but this initial program was attracting students from other states.

Moody did clinical work at Mercy Hospital in Grand Rapids, Minnesota, and returned to Minneapolis to work at area hospitals and to teach part-time in the Nurse Anesthesia program at Abbott Northwestern. Like many others who later joined the faculty of the Saint Mary's Schools of Graduate and Professional Programs (SGPP), Moody considered the Nurse Anesthesia program with Abbott Northwestern to be the critical first step in transitioning from an undergraduate, residential college to a full-fledged university. By the time she began working full-time for the Nurse Anesthesia program as clinical director, the program had a new address.

Moody recalled her first encounter with Brother Louis in the mid-1990s. She had urged Saint Mary's to acquire the entire Nurse Anesthesia program from Abbott Northwestern Hospital. Saint Mary's was definitely taking a risk, but Brother Louis, never adverse to risk, replied, "Unless your money is out taking risks, you're never going to gain anything." He wholeheartedly supported the acquisition, and Abbott Northwestern Hospital exited 2500 Park Avenue once the two parties signed the contracts in the spring of 1997. The Nurse Anesthesia program expanded through a series of hospital partnerships statewide. St. Paul's Ramsey Hospital closed its program and offered it to Saint Mary's.

One of the oldest partnerships was with Owatonna Hospital, and a newer one was with the Marshfield Clinic. Saint Mary's added more rural hospitals in Wabasha, Lake City, and Forest Lake. Duluth came next, with its St. Mary's, Miller-Dwan, and St. Luke's; then the hospital in Marshall, Minnesota, signed on. Saint Mary's soon found itself with 26 hospitals and 36 students.

2500 Park Avenue

The building at 2500 Park Avenue had seen better days when Saint Mary's negotiated an agreement in the mid-1980s to lease classroom and office space on the second floor. South of downtown Minneapolis at East 25th Street and near the intersection of I-94 and I-35W, the building had once been at the center of a bustling residential area for captains of industry who made Minneapolis a thriving business community with banks, grain elevators, and lumber mills. By 1985, the Phillips neighborhood was a rundown collection of rental housing and small shops catering to Hennepin County's poorest residents. Because Phillips was also the foremost immigrant neighborhood in the Twin Cities, the Saint Mary's location served a new generation of Minnesotans who wanted further education.

Barbara Croucher, currently director of administration at the Twin Cities campus of Saint Mary's University, recalled approaching the side door of 2500 Park Avenue in 1985 for a job interview with some trepidation, not all of it about the interview. She came to the door, marked as 2510 Park Avenue, but with no sign. A stairway led up to the reception desk with its Saint Mary's logo. After she was hired, she and 10 other staff members wore many hats, answering telephones, emptying wastebaskets, and shopping for supplies. About 100 students were enrolled. Saint Mary's had recently transferred its graduate programs from Cretin High School and St. John's Hospital in St. Paul. Students at Park Avenue had several program options, including Nurse Anesthesia, Psychology, and Human Development.

Graduate Program Expansion

Between 1985 and 1992, the Minneapolis graduate programs had explosive growth. Under the leadership of Vice President Dr. Suzanne James, Academic Dean Brother Julius Winkler (academic dean in Winona in the 1950s and 1960s), and the second academic dean, Dr. Marilyn Frost, enrollment steadily increased to more than 1,000 students, most of them adults working during the day and attending class in the evening. Recognizing the different set of students in Minneapolis, Saint Mary's made every effort to accommodate them. The academic infrastructure featured an integrated curriculum in outreach locations taught by adjunct professors during worker-friendly hours.

The programs had little competition, because Saint Mary's was ahead of the adult learning curve and was mission-driven. Tuition was at a level that many, if not most, students could afford. The main theme is that Saint Mary's was successful in responding to adult learners; a subsidiary theme is that the programs were unencumbered by traditional academic structures and bureaucracy.

The staff attributed the success to the vision of Brother Louis, who nurtured the graduate programs with his entrepreneurial spirit and his notion of tailoring education for adult students. The people working with the graduate programs wholeheartedly believed in the mission; theirs was a labor of love.

The 1990s were years of continued strong enrollment growth and of graduate program expansion. The goals of a successful, record-breaking, $12.5-million capital campaign by Saint Mary's University included improvements to the Park Avenue building in Minneapolis and construction of a residence hall for 60 students on the Winona campus. At the time, Saint Mary's University operated three

Merri Moody, a Saint Mary's University student, teacher, and administrator since the mid-1980s, is program director and associate professor in the M.S. in Nurse Anesthesia program and dean of the Graduate School of Health and Human Services.

Sister Mary Lonan Reilly, OSF, and Sister Michaea Byron, OSF, president of the College of Saint Teresa, and Brother Louis DeThomasis, president of Saint Mary's College, at a 1986 reception.

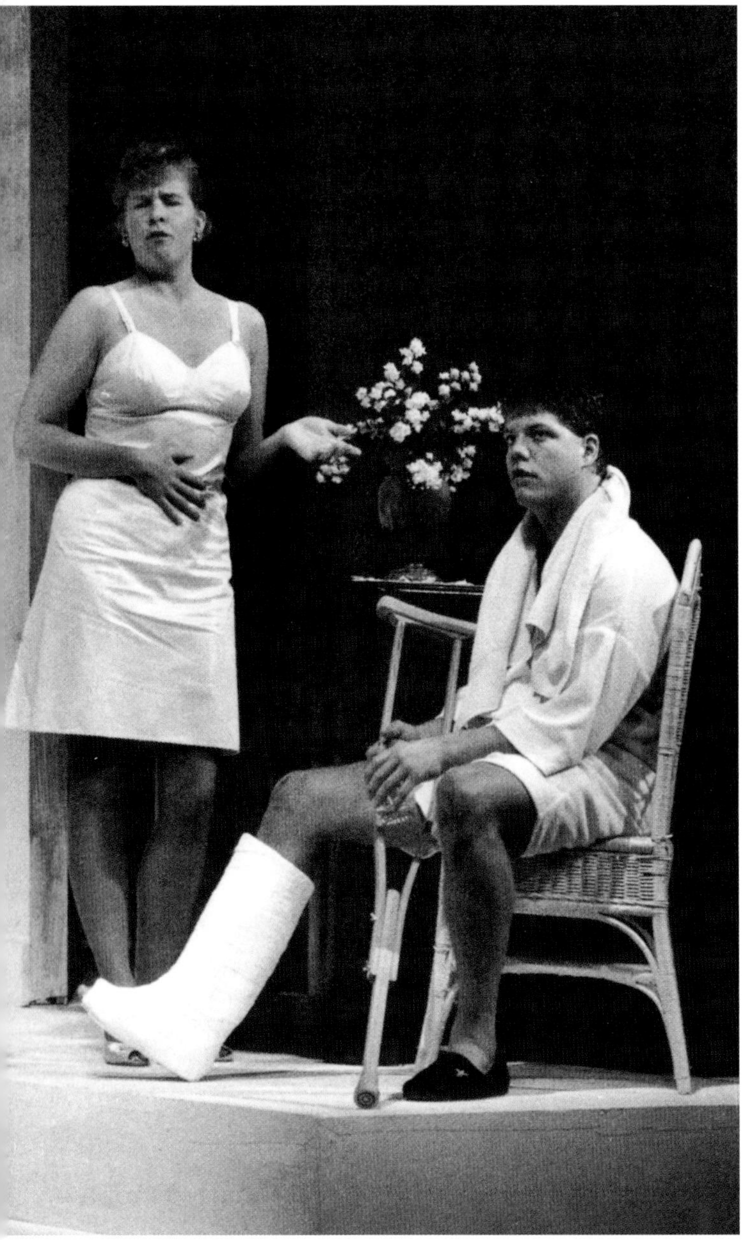

Tom Monaghan, founder of Domino's Pizza, spoke to a business class in Saint Mary's Hall in 1989.

In 1989, the Saint Mary's College Theatre Department presented Cat on a Hot Tin Roof, *by Tennessee Williams, at the Joseph Page Theatre in the Performance Center.*

centers: the Terrace Heights campus in Winona, the Minneapolis Graduate Center on Park Avenue, and the satellite Graduate Center at Rochester Technical College in Rochester, Minnesota.

In a 1991 interview, Dr. Susan Huber, dean of continuing education, summed up the Saint Mary's commitment in Minneapolis. "The philosophy of the Christian Brothers is to bring education to the people," Huber said. "That's what we're doing."

In 1991, enrollment in the graduate programs in Minneapolis and in Rochester was about 2,500 students, with an average age of 37. Most of the 175 faculty members were adjunct professors. The Minneapolis Graduate Center offered 11 programs. To encourage class discussion and as much teacher contact as possible, class size was limited to 25 students.

Student character and motivation impressed the faculty and staff. Many students were immigrants from Somalia, Russia, Eastern Europe, and Myanmar. Almost everyone was the first one in the family to attend college. All juggled work and family life with study.

The graduate offerings on the Winona campus also were growing, for example, in arts administration. The major new initiative in Minneapolis in 1991 was the decision to offer the bachelor's and the master's degrees in telecommunications at corporate campuses in the Twin Cities area. The telecommunications initiative that began in 1987 at 2500 Park Avenue was a visionary program. Few people at the time even knew what telecommunications meant.

In the early 1990s, the Bachelor's Completion program drove much of the growth. More and more of the Fortune 500 companies headquartered in the Twin Cities were requiring their employees to have a college degree. Saint Mary's recognized the trend and began offering courses to help employees complete the bachelor's degree in a non-traditional way.

Bob Anderson, the founding father of the Bachelor's Completion program and the director of

information technology at Northwest Airlines, was teaching in the master's in Telecommunications program. During the 1989–90 academic year, he proposed a program to help his employees complete the bachelor's degree. He adopted a model developed at Regis College in Denver. Saint Mary's offered the first class in 1991, at Northwest Airlines, and added Norstan, Inc. in Plymouth, Minnesota, as a site. Saint Mary's added the Bachelor of Science programs in Business, Marketing, Human Resource Management, and Political Science.

In the late 1990s, the Graduate Center further evolved to serve employer needs by adding more courses; everything blossomed after 2000. One arrangement was with Dunwoody Institute for a B.S. in Industrial Management. Bachelor's Completion was a powerful initiative that allowed Saint Mary's University to work with adult learners in a new way.

Psychology is another graduate program that expanded rapidly after 1995. Developed in the 1970s by Brother Julius Winkler, by the early 1990s it was one of the more popular offerings. Licensing rules had changed in the 1990s, and students were working on M.A.'s in Psychology at the time, because if they started their courses by 1991, they could be licensed as a psychologist.

Wisconsin native Dr. Christina Huck, director since June 1994, had charge of the Psychology program that was growing by leaps and bounds. The Licensed Psychological Practitioner, Licensed Professional Counselor, and Licensed Professional Clinical Counselor programs added more options for students. Next came the Marriage and Family Certification program and the M.A. in Marriage and Family Therapy. Students in these programs increasingly went on to doctoral programs at the University of Minnesota and the University of St. Thomas.

The 21 years between Brother Louis' arrival in 1984 and his decision to retire as president of Saint Mary's University in 2005 is a dynamic period similar to the founding decades of Saint Mary's College. The transformation of Saint Mary's University continues in the 21st century on the basis of the groundwork that positioned the university to remain a faithful, creative leader within the network of Lasallian schools and universities.

Transition to New Leadership

The Board of Trustees turned to Brother Craig Franz to lead the university in 2005. After Brother Craig's resignation in December 2006, the board asked Brother Louis DeThomasis to reassume the duties of president while the search continued for a new president.

In 2008, the board appointed Brother William Mann the 13th president of Saint Mary's University of Minnesota. A New York native, Brother William spent much of his career as an administrator. He served in Rome from 2000 to 2007 as the vicar general of the Institute of the Brothers of the Christian Schools, helping to oversee the regions and districts responsible for nearly 1,000 Lasallian schools in 82 countries. He already was known

Cross-country skiing on the Saint Mary's University of Minnesota trail network designed and groomed by Brother Jerome Rademacher and his colleagues is a popular winter activity on the Winona campus.

Saint Mary's University of Minnesota expanded the Music Department and its performing ensembles in the 1980s and 1990s with new facilities in the Performance Center and in St. Yon Hall.

at Saint Mary's University, having been a member of the Board of Trustees from 1996 to 2001.

Brother William arrived with the mission to continue transforming Saint Mary's University of Minnesota as it approached its second century. He had a platform of success on which to build, but his arrival in Minnesota came amidst the worst economic problems the state and the nation had experienced since the Great Depression. The Winona campus was thriving and providing an international university education to women and men on a traditional residential campus. In 2007, the year before Brother William took office, Saint Mary's University of Minnesota renewed its accreditation by the North Central Association of Colleges and Schools.

The Hendrickson Institute for Ethical Leadership, founded in 1994, and its public programs in the Twin Cities enhanced the status of Saint Mary's University. The Kabara Institute for Entrepreneurial Studies, established with the vision of Dr. Jon '48 and Betty Kabara, the First-Generation Initiative, the Lasallian Studies Institute and Master of Arts, and the purchase of the Prairie Island Field Station added to the university's

growing reputation for cutting-edge thinking and educational expertise.

The graduate campus in the Twin Cities enrolled more than 4,000 students, making Saint Mary's University of Minnesota one of the largest graduate schools in the state. Adult education grew from the leased space on Park Avenue in Minneapolis to a multi-site, multi-country educational network of Bachelor's Completion, graduate degree, and professional development programs. Much of that growth occurred during the early 2000s as a result of the university's ability to seize opportunities to serve adult learners.

Satellite Centers

During the 1990s, Minneapolis and St. Paul experienced a demographic trend of growth in the suburbs at the expense of the inner city. Increasingly, companies located headquarters or major divisions in suburbs such as Apple Valley, Minnetonka, Oakdale, and dozens of other thriving locales. The young professionals working in those suburban office centers increasingly lived in the same suburbs. In the Lasallian tradition of going where the need is, Saint Mary's University concentrated on a plan to bring graduate education to adult learners in the suburbs.

This 1992 aerial view shows the Saint Mary's campus in Winona, prior to the construction of many buildings and facilities.

In June 2007, in an old city hall and police station, the university opened its Apple Valley Center, one of its fastest-growing facilities, in partnership with Dakota County Technical College (DCTC) and Inver Hills Community College (IHCC). The City of Apple Valley owns the building; DCTC leases it and subleases space to Saint Mary's University and to IHCC. An average of 550 Saint Mary's students each semester attend class at the Apple Valley Center; more than 600 students registered for the fall 2011 semester for classes in the Bachelor's Completion and graduate degree programs, as well as the weekend programs administered by the Winona campus. Saint Mary's has 11 classrooms at Apple Valley, and classes average no more than 25 students. SGPP staff believes that if the university had five or six more classrooms at Apple Valley, enrollment would be at capacity within a semester. Core courses in management and for the MBA program are the most popular, along with courses in the Educational Leadership program.

Bringing Bachelor's Completion to the West Metro

The west metro area of the Twin Cities has a high percentage of Fortune 500 companies whose employees have at least a bachelor's degree. Saint Mary's University helps employees without a bachelor's degree pursue one through the Bachelor's Completion program. The university opened its Minnetonka Center in 2008 to fill that need. The Minnetonka Center offers the Bachelor's Completion program to General Mills, Cargill, Target, and other corporate employees.

Ian Pannkuk, a 2006 Saint Mary's University graduate, worked in the university's Admissions Department,

transferred to the Twin Cities campus, moved to the Minnetonka Center, and in 2012 transferred to the university's Pathways Program, which works closely with community colleges in the metro area to help adult learners transfer smoothly to the various Saint Mary's University offerings.

Anna (Shields '04) Reichers oversees the university's Oakdale Center, which in the fall of 2011 enrolled 200 students in various programs, mostly in certificate and degree programs in education offered at other Saint Mary's centers. The Oakdale Center draws students from the east metro, Stillwater, and Hudson, Wisconsin. As at Minnetonka, much of the work is with bachelor's completion. Because of the nearby 3M Corporation, the availability of graduate courses makes the Bachelor's Completion program all the more attractive. The Oakdale Center partners with Inver Hills Community College.

Expanding Statewide

Through SGPP, Saint Mary's University of Minnesota has had a surprising influence on education in Minnesota. Many of the state's school superintendents and principals attained their positions through the university's licensure programs.

An example of the staff who work in the licensure programs is Sarah (Fisher '04) Wanger, a Saint Mary's graduate and Theatre major, who in 2006 began at SGPP as an administrative assistant and quickly became an admissions counselor working with educators who want to advance in their careers. Most of the people she helps are teachers who want to pursue licensure or a master's degree. Saint Mary's works with its students to make classwork as flexible as possible. Most programs are cohort-based and offered across the state, from Duluth and the Iron Range to Marshall and Worthington. In

This most recent aerial view of the Winona campus includes residence halls, public spaces, and academic and athletic facilities constructed since 1992. Not visible to the right is Brother Leopold Hall, a residence hall added in 2012.

Adult Bachelor's Completion graduates cherish the memory of commencement ceremonies.

Saint Mary's University's SGPP graduates during a 2008 ceremony.

the 2011–12 academic year, for example, the university recruited its 29th St. Cloud cohort.

Saint Mary's University offers two-week summer courses on the Twin Cities campus and is increasingly enabling students to do online learning. An increasing number of people are making mid-career changes, and SGPP counselors are helping them pursue career goals and navigate the daunting world of financial aid. Saint Mary's counselors emphasize that the university strives to keep education affordable and accessible, in the tradition of Saint John Baptist de La Salle and the early Brothers.

The ongoing expansion of the SGPP will be guided by its Council of Regents. The Council is made up of Twin Cities-area leaders committed to sustaining and advancing Saint Mary's personalized, high-quality graduate and degree completion programs by providing valuable expertise and advice to the university.

A Place to Call Home

The undergraduate students who enrolled at Saint Mary's University of Minnesota in Winona in the fall of 2011 was the last class to begin during the university's first century

The Schools of Graduate and Professional Programs' (SGPP) Apple Valley Center occupies the Twin Cities suburb's former municipal building.

In the tradition of Brother Charles Severin, Saint Mary's University faculty and students study the environment of planet Earth.

of existence. The undergraduate experience of those young men and women has in many ways changed dramatically since the first class enrolled in 1913. In many other ways, the traditions of the Terrace Heights campus amidst the bluffs of the Mississippi River Valley are a reminder that the more things change, the more they remain the same.

Winona students, in a roundtable discussion in the fall of 2011, talked about their love of the small campus, the southeastern Minnesota location, the campus community, and the Lasallian tradition. They liked the fact that teachers know their students and are always accessible and willing to listen to them. The school is small enough to allow participation in extracurricular activities, and they are impressed that Saint Mary's University is preparing them to enter today's workforce as it has been doing for the generations of students before them.

Students have their complaints, mostly about the food, as in previous generations, but by and large, they feel part of a nurturing, welcoming community. "Saint Mary's is my second home," said one student from La Crosse, Wisconsin. "It's the place that I call home."

The university hopes to tell that same story in the decades ahead as it builds on its past and launches a strategic planning process to shape its future for the next 100 years. Town hall meetings, focus groups, and discussions have engaged people in conversations whose transformative power will be both the cause and effect of strategic planning.

Strategic planning has brought to the surface what people think Saint Mary's University of Minnesota will look like in a decade or two. "What's the next step?" Brother William asks. "We're trying to tell stories to illustrate that next step."

- † Stories about a visionary bishop, a century ago, who decided to build a complete network of Catholic education in his southern Minnesota diocese and established the men's college in Winona to complete the job.
- † Stories about the De La Salle Christian Brothers, who saw an opportunity to establish their Scholasticate at Saint Mary's College and to educate thousands of young men from Chicago and the Midwest in the Lasallian tradition.
- † Stories about the pioneering young women, many of them the daughters, sisters, and cousins of Saint Mary's and Saint Teresa alums, who transformed Saint Mary's College in the 1970s and 1980s and fostered the Lasallian mission in the process.
- † Stories about the Brother Charles Severin Award winners and other outstanding faculty, such as Dr. Richard Kowles, Dr. Clyde Kendrick, Dr. Pat Costello, Dr. Blanche Premo, and others who contributed to the reputation of Saint Mary's University for educational rigor and excellence.
- † Stories about the transition in the 1980s and 1990s from the college to the university that in the finest Lasallian tradition brought education to adult learners of the Twin Cities and outstate Minnesota.

These are the stories that Brother William thinks will promise and create a bright future for Saint Mary's University of Minnesota in the next 100 years.

Saint Mary's global footprint has expanded to include the Maryknoll Institute for African Studies and Christ the Teacher Institute for Education (CTIE), both in Nairobi, and a partnership with the Catholic College of Mandeville in Jamaica.

The 2006 graduates of Christ the Teacher Institute for Education (CTIE), Nairobi, Kenya, affiliated with Saint Mary's University.

Brother Louis DeThomasis, FSC
11th President, 1984–2005

Because of his lengthy and innovative tenure as president, Brother Louis DeThomasis, FSC, had a transforming impact on Saint Mary's University of Minnesota.

A native of Bethpage, Long Island, New York, Brother Louis attended public grade school and the Christian Brothers' La Salle Military Academy. He enrolled at Georgetown University in Washington, D.C., in the fall of 1958. After earning a bachelor's degree at the School of Foreign Service, he spent a year studying at the University of Madrid. After returning to the United States in 1964 and working as a businessman and entrepreneur for a few years, he entered the novitiate of the Long Island-New England District at the age of 26. He became a school administrator, including headmaster at La Salle Military Academy, and in 1981 he started Christian Brothers Investment Services, Inc., which currently manages $4 billion of invested funds for Catholic dioceses, schools, hospitals, and organizations. He earned a Ph.D. in Financial Management from the Union Institute.

In 1984, the Board of Trustees appointed Brother Louis the 11th president of Saint Mary's College. Intending to be an agent of change, he presided over dramatic innovation in his more than 21 years as president. He transformed a small, liberal arts, residential college with a graduate program of 200 students into an international, multi-campus, undergraduate, graduate, post-graduate, and doctoral university of more than 4,000 students. He brought Lasallian education to underserved adult students in Minnesota and oversaw the transformation of Saint Mary's College into Saint Mary's University of Minnesota in 1995.

Brother Louis continued the construction activity of his predecessors, adding or expanding more than 14 buildings on the Winona and Minneapolis campuses during his presidency.

The Saint Mary's University women's fastpitch softball team won the 2000 NCAA Division III National Championship.

Brother William Mann, president, greeted parents and grandparents at Saint Mary's Family Weekend.

The Saint Teresa Leadership and Service Institute for women embraces Franciscan, Teresan, and Lasallian values.

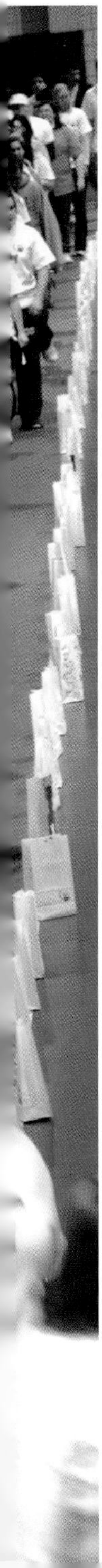

More than 300 Saint Mary's University students, faculty, and staff raise $17,000 or more for the American Cancer Society during the Relay for Life each March, walking overnight on the indoor track in Gostomski Fieldhouse.

Saint Mary's University students in 2011 moved into residence halls at the start of another academic year.

The Oakdale Center of Saint Mary's University serves students in the Twin Cities east metro and as far as Stillwater and Bayport.

The Hendrickson Institute for Ethical Leadership is committed to developing aspiring and current leaders to lives of ethical leadership and service. The annual Hendrickson Forum recognizes ethical local leaders and features international keynote speakers like Sue Gardner of Wikimedia Foundation in 2012.

The Minnetonka Center serves adult learners in the western suburbs of the Twin Cities.

Linka Holey, associate vice president and academic dean of SGPP, is in her third decade with Saint Mary's.

Brother Craig Franz, FSC
12th President, 2005–2006

Brother Craig Franz, FSC became the 12th president of Saint Mary's University in June 2005, after serving as president of Saint Mary's College of California, Moraga, since 1997. During his eight years as president of Saint Mary's College of California, he was a member of the Board of Trustees of Saint Mary's University of Minnesota.

Brother Craig earned a Bachelor of Science in Biology at Bucknell University in 1975, a Master of Science in Environmental Studies at Drexel University in 1977, and a Ph.D. in Biology and Marine Ecology at the University of Rhode Island in 1988.

He began his career as a high school biology and environmental science teacher in Lasallian schools in Philadelphia and taught and held administrative posts at the University of Rhode Island and La Salle University, Philadelphia.

In 1994, Brother Craig came to Winona as executive assistant to the president and dean of the School of Mathematics and Science of Saint Mary's University of Minnesota. He taught Marine Ecology and directed the university's international programs in London, Mexico City, Nairobi, and Italy.

As president, Brother Craig issued the challenge to make Saint Mary's University of Minnesota a nationally recognized teaching institution by its centennial year, 2012. Undergraduate and graduate enrollment increased during his presidency, and the university purchased a new building for the Minneapolis graduate center. Brother Craig was the founding president of the International Association of Lasallian Universities (IALU), a global consortium of Lasallian universities that promotes excellence in Catholic higher education among 65 member universities.

A Somali family celebrated after the graduation ceremony at the Saint Mary's University campus in Minneapolis.

The first three graduates in 2012 of the Master of Arts in Lasallian Leadership program.

Dr. Marilyn Frost advised students at the Saint Mary's College Graduate Center in the late 1980s.

The Rochester Center of Saint Mary's University continues the graduate work begun in Rochester in the 1950s.

Brother William Mann, FSC

13th President, 2008

Brother William Mann, FSC became the 13th president of Saint Mary's University of Minnesota in 2008. In selecting him, the Board of Trustees reached back to the New York roots of Brother Peter Clifford and Brother Louis DeThomasis, who guided the university from 1976 onward.

A native of Brooklyn, New York, Brother William earned a B.A. in Literature at The Catholic University of America, an M.A. in Liberal Studies at the State University of New York–Stony Brook, an M.A. in Spirituality at Salve Regina University in Rhode Island, and a Doctor of Ministry in Family Ministry at Colgate Rochester Divinity School.

From 2000 to 2007, Brother William was the vicar general of the Institute of the Brothers of the Christian Schools, which has 5,300 Brothers working in association with 73,000 men and women educators in the operation of 930 schools and universities that serve over 900,000 students in 82 countries.

As president, Brother William has focused significant energies in a variety of areas. In the area of attention to the university's Lasallian Catholic heritage, numerous employees have participated in Lasallian formation programs at the international, regional, and local level. In addition, Brother William inaugurated the Institute of Lasallian Studies, the *AXIS* journal, and the Symposium on Lasallian Research. He inaugurated the Cardinal Conversation on issues related to the university's Catholic heritage. Brother William also established the First-Generation Initiative and Countdown to College.

In the area of academic excellence, the Higher Learning Commission has granted the university permission to create a second doctorate, the Psy.D., and the university is partnering with Deltak on fully online graduate degrees. In the area of facilities, the Saint Mary's University Center in the Twin Cities (three buildings) was purchased and is being renovated. La Salle Hall and the Saint Thomas More Chapel were renovated. The track and soccer field construction was completed, as was Brother Leopold Hall, a new residence hall on the Winona campus.

Finally, Brother William initiated the creation of the Human Resources Department for the university. He also established advisory boards for various university institutes and schools, allowing the university to engage more significantly with alumni.

At the Twin Cities campus, buildings purchased in 2011 are being transformed into a versatile Saint Mary's University Center for multiple uses.

Staff hosted an open house at the Apple Valley Center of Saint Mary's University.

The Saint Thomas More Chapel on the Winona campus, refurbished in the spring of 2012.

The Park Avenue North building is one of several additions to the Twin Cities campus of Saint Mary's University since the move to 2500 Park Avenue in 1984.

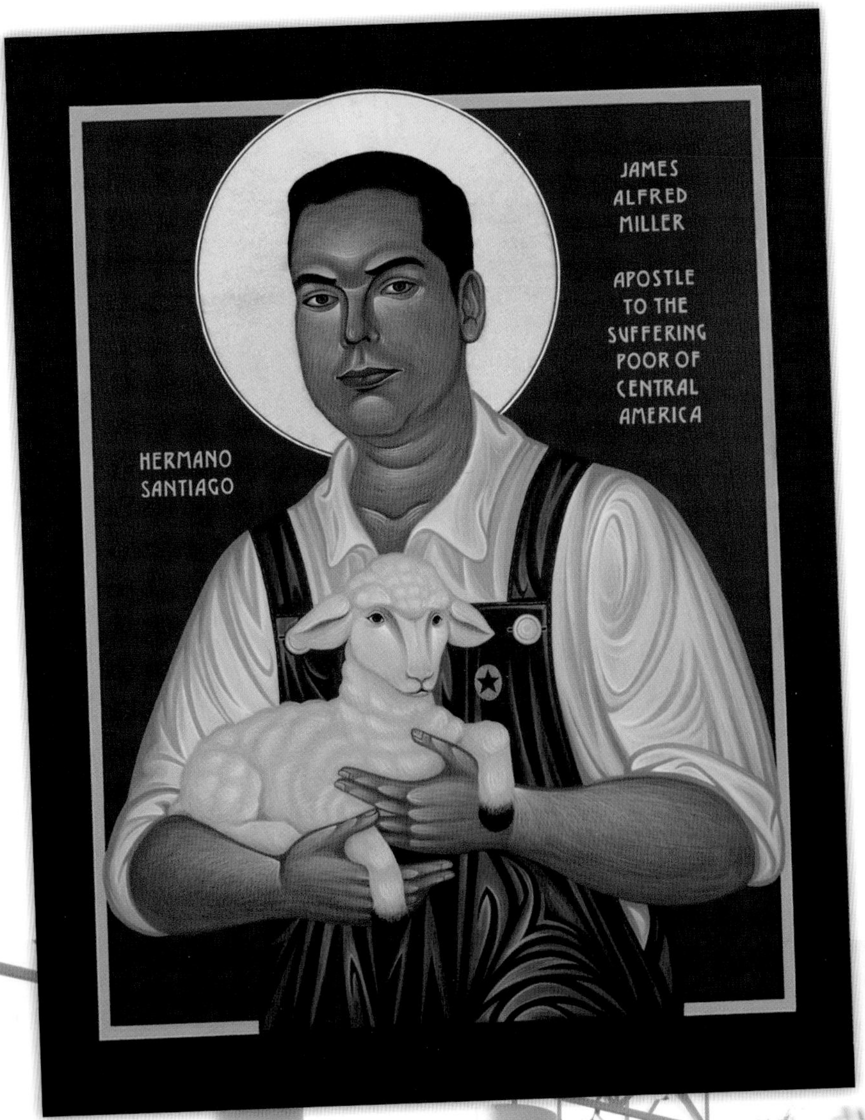

Brother James Alfred Miller, FSC '66, was killed in 1982 while doing mission work with the poor in Guatemala. He is pictured in an icon published by the Christian Brothers of the Midwest District.

After torrential rains flood Rushford, Minnesota, in August 2007, Saint Mary's University students helped the community recover from the disaster.

The Cardinal mascot leads freshmen in cheers as Saint Mary's University celebrated its centennial year and its 85th year in the Minnesota Intercollegiate Athletic Conference (MIAC).

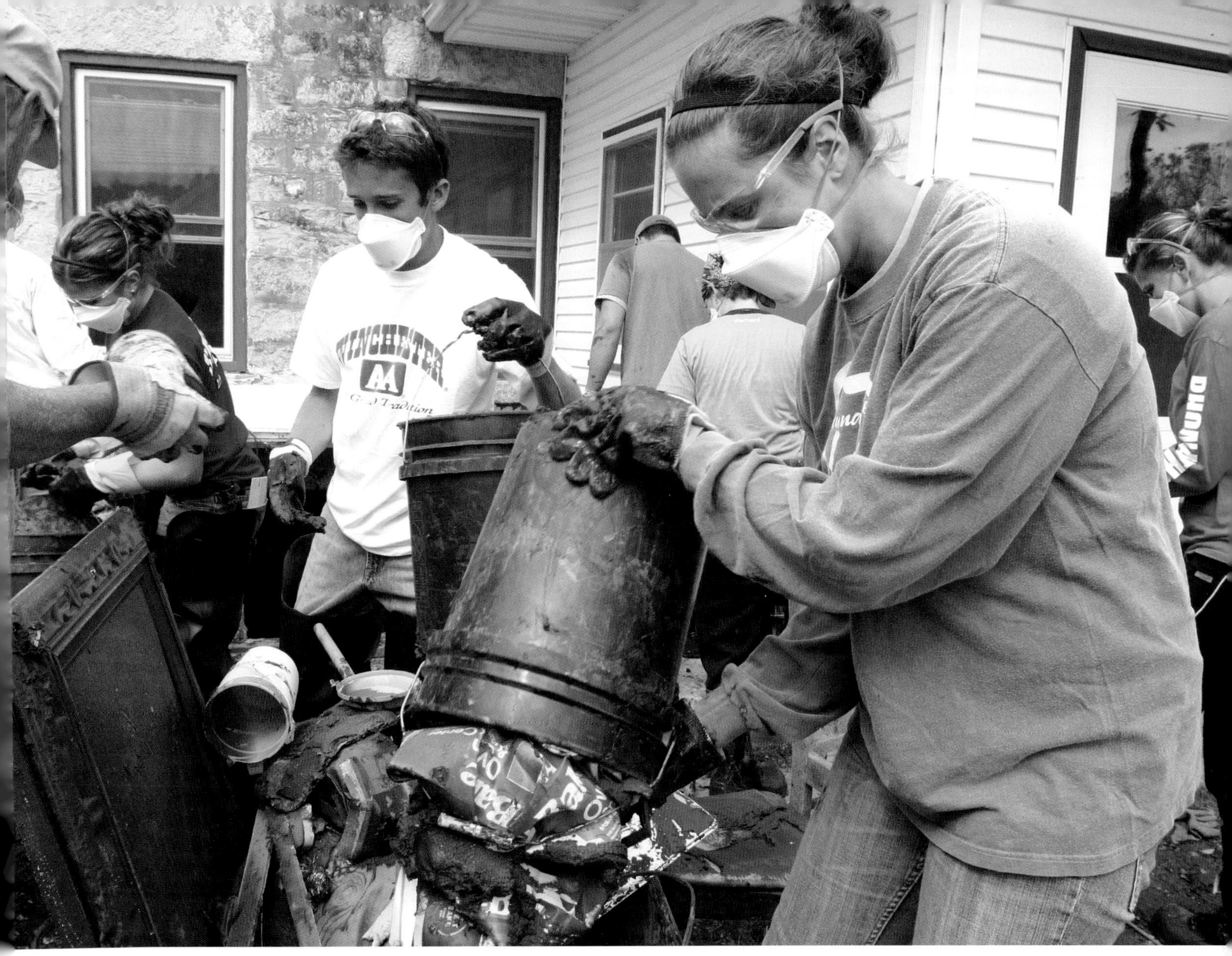

First-Generation Initiative scholars are provided with opportunities designed to provide college access and success to students from underserved communities.

In the late 1990s, the SGPP of Saint Mary's University expanded along Park Avenue South in Minneapolis.

Brother Larry Humphrey, director of mission, shared a light moment with Saint Mary's University students in 2007.

Father Andrew Fabian has taught in the Philosophy Department since 1964. In the centennial year of 2012 he was awarded the Presidential Award for Outstanding Merit.

The Twin Cities campus includes La Salle Hall (opposite) and Martin de Porres Hall (left).

Students with Brother William, president, by Saint Mary's Hall create a timeless image to commemorate the first century of Saint Mary's University of Minnesota.

Brother Fredy Peredin, Brother John Grover '65, and Brother Frank Walsh '45 renewed their vows in honor of their jubilees.

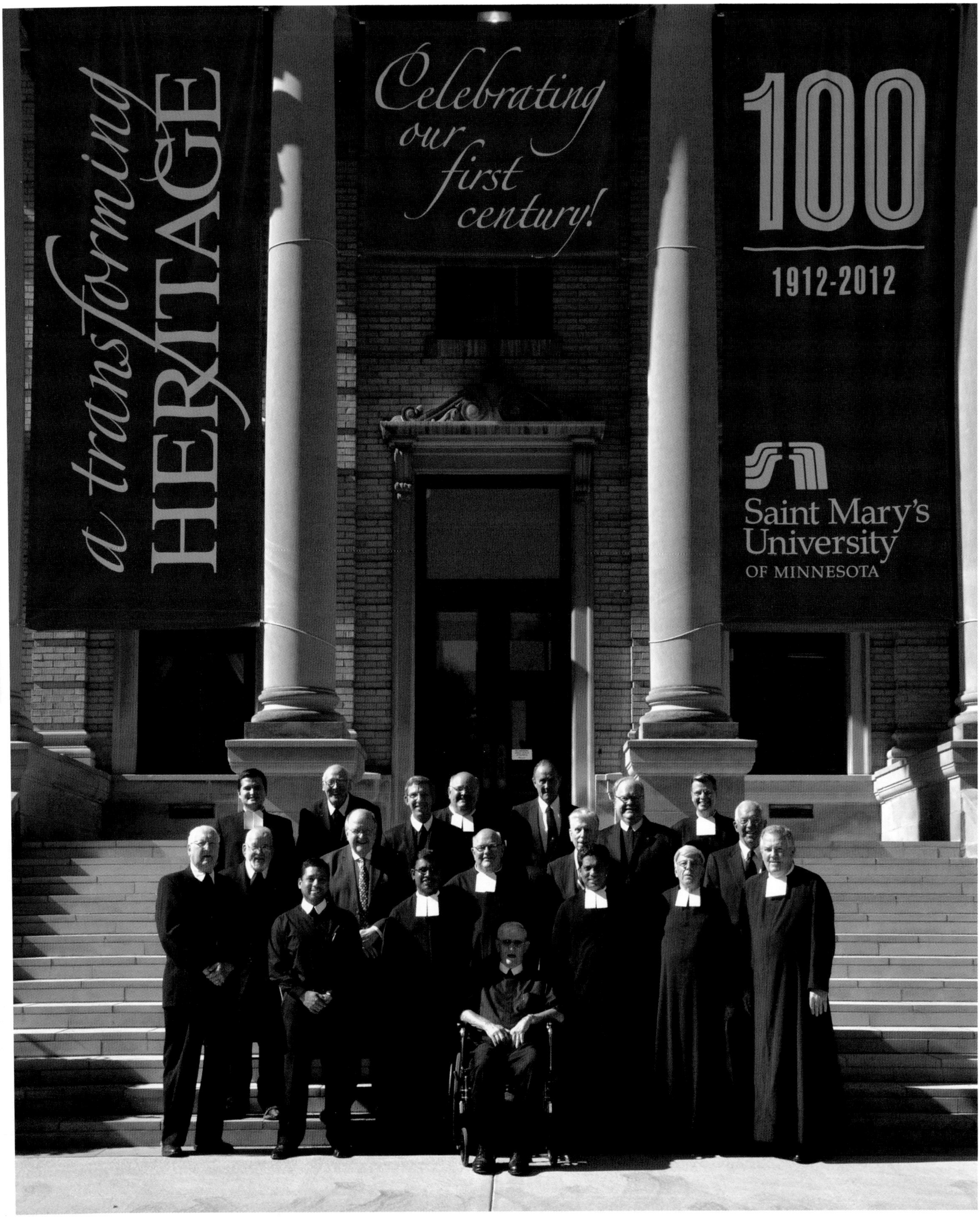

Christian Brothers in residence at Saint Mary's in the fall of 2012 were, front: Brother Frank Walsh '45; first row (from left): Brother Edward Everett '50, Brother Miguel Mendoza, Brother Christy Croos M '13, Brother Fredy Peredin M '13, Brother Stephen Rusyn, and Brother William Mann; second row: Brother Finbar McMullen '46, Brother Roderick Robertson '63, Brother Francis Carr '66, Brother Charles Burke '57, and Brother Damian Steger '58, M '91; third row: Brother Diego Rico M '13, Brother Arnold McMullen '53, Brother Edmund Siderewicz, Brother Lawrence Humphrey, Brother John Grover '65, Brother Thomas Houde, and Brother Patrick Conway '75.

PRESIDENTIAL AWARD FOR OUTSTANDING MERIT

2012	Father Andrew Fabian, OP
	Richard V. Kowles M '67, Ph.D.
2011	Brother I. Basil Rothweiler '38, FSC
2010	John F. McDonough '75
	Sister Una O'Connor, CP
2009	Dr. John M. Domanico '77
2007	Brother Paul Joslin, FSC
	Brother Martin Spellman '54, FSC

BROTHER H. CHARLES SEVERIN AWARD FOR EXCELLENCE IN TEACHING

2011	Melissa Luedtke, Ed.D.
2009	Dean Beckman, M.S.
2007	Preston Lawing, M.F.A.
2005	Marilyn Frost, Ph.D.
2003	Jane Kelley Rodeheffer, Ph.D.
2001	Jay D. Mutter, Ph.D.
1999	Jeffrey Hefel, M.B.A.
1997	Donald J. Peake, Ph.D.
1995	John J. Johnson, Ph.D.
1993	Brother Arnold McMullen, FSC
1992	Stanley Pollock, Ph.D.
1991	Larry Luttmers, Ph.D.
1990	Andrea Birch, Ph.D.
1989	John Morgan, Ph.D.
1987	Vincent Colapietro, Ph.D.
1986	Arthur Spring, Ph.D.
1985	Brother Jerome Rademacher, FSC, Ph.D.
1984	Patrick Costello, Ph.D.
1983	Paul Froeschl, Ph.D.
1982	Father Andrew Fabian, OP, Ph.L.
1981	Brother Raphael Erler, FSC, Ph.D.
1980	Richard Kowles, Ph.D.
1979	Marietta Conroy, Ph.D.

DISTINGUISHED LASALLIAN EDUCATOR AWARD

2012	Mary Catherine Fox, Ph.D.
2011	Roxanne Eubank, Ed.D.
2010	Brother Stephen Rusyn, FSC, Ph.D.
2009	Jane Anderson, Ph.D.
2000	Brother Louis DeThomasis, FSC, Ph.D.
1992	Brother Jerome Rademacher, FSC, Ph.D.
1988	Jeff Highland, Ph.D.

BROTHER LOUIS DeTHOMASIS, FSC AWARD

2011	Christina Huck, Ph.D.

BISHOP PATRICK HEFFRON AWARD FOR SERVICE

2012	Roger Peckover, Ph.D.
2010	Mary Becker
2008	Alan Joswick
2006	Linka Holey
2004	Francis Speck
2002	Brother Jerome Rademacher, FSC, Ph.D.
2000	Kenneth Pellegrini
1998	Darlene C. Paulson
1996	Joan M. Costello
1994	Marilyn Frost, Ph.D.
1993	Anthony M. Piscitiello
1992	Brother John Grover, FSC
1991	Jeffrey R. Highland, Ph.D.
1990	James Hanzel
1989	Helen Galloway, Ph.D.
	Brother Francis Walsh, FSC, Ph.D.
1987	Brother Leonard Courtney, FSC, Ph.D.
1986	Brother Paul Grass, FSC, Ph.D.
1985	Kathryn P. McDermott
	Robert F. McDermott
1984	Christian Brothers of SMC
1983	William Ammentorp, Ph.D.
1982	Reverend Robert Taylor
	Monsignor Bernard Mangan
1980	Brother J. Leo Northam, FSC
1979	Monsignor Roy E. Literski, Ph.D.
1976	Brother George Pahl, FSC, Ph.D.
1973	C. Bernard Jacobs
1970	Dr. Jon J. Kabara
	Father Paul Nelson
1969	John D. Lamon
	Brother H. Charles Severin, FSC, Ph.D.
	A. J. McGill
1968	Monsignor J. Stanley Hale
	Brother Leopold J. Dodd, FSC
	Michael Galvin
	Thomas Coughlan
1967	Frank D. Biesanz
	Rt. Reverend Monsignor Ambrose Layne
	Judge E. D. Libera
1966	John A. Metcalf
	Joseph C. Page
	Thomas H. Skemp
1965	Charles P. Biesanz
	Reverend Frank McMahon
	Rt. Reverend Monsignor Julius Haun
	Rt. Reverend Monsignor Bernard Kramer
1964	Walter E. Kelly, Sr.

OUTSTANDING SENIORS

2012	Michael Mochler, Regina Quandt
2011	Sean Ohl, Hilary Ethen
2010	David Dahlstrom, Mariana Sanchez
2009	Jakub Szymanski, Emily Berg
2008	Kevin Black, Anastacia Sontag
2007	Davey Warner, Sarah Bellingham
2006	Dominic Lawrence, Sara Vargason
2005	Liam O'Farrell, Ashley Dingels
2004	Nathan Semsch, Jennifer Lawrence
2003	Nicholas Michaels, Elizabeth McDowell
2002	Douglas Werner, Katie LaPlant
2001	Nathan Albee, Ann Durley
2000	Corey Sievers, Sarah Bayer
1999	Andrew Yori, Jennifer Paul
1998	Jesse Murray, Kathryn Vandenberg
1997	Trent Vorlicek, Sarah Jorgensen
1996	Benjamin Murray, Elizabeth Kress
1995	Brandon Sitzman, Julie Dahlheimer
1994	Steven Snyder, Amy Kazlauskas
1993	Thomas Cook, Jennifer Hurley
1992	Steve Beaudry, Molly Guest
1991	Joseph Tadie, Amy Smith
1990	Christopher Higgins, Julie Carroll
1989	James Chatto, Peggy Powell
1988	Michael Majerus, Eileen Gibbons
1987	Walter Jungbauer, Ann Christensen
1986	Gordon Hannon, Elizabeth Enderle
1985	Luke Osterhaus, Patricia Rice
1984	Phil Kluesner, Kirsten Almo
1983	Mark Steinke, Maureen Forsythe
1982	Stephen Glynn, Anne Broghammer
1981	Paul Mulcahy, Patricia Leonard
1980	Joseph Phillips, Maureen Milligan
1979	Louis McCoy, Kathleen Scherek
1978	Kevin Cushing, Linda Kuczma
1977	Robert Rettig, Jacinta Timmons/Andre Carlevato
1976	John Halpin, Mary Ann Gay
1975	Edward Lawson, Michelle Langenderfer
1974	William Crimmins, Christina Prusank
1973	Tom Rodell, Mary Lucas
1972	Robert Cern
1971	Jeff Ulanski
1970	Thomas Murray
1969	Tony Piscitiello
1968	Marty O'Sullivan
1967	Ralph Zito
1966	Terrence Truhler
1965	Bud Seall
1964	Paul Meyer
1963	Charles Wheeler
1962	Richard Caldwell

DISTINGUISHED ALUMNI

2012	Dr. Roger Lucas '65
2011	Dr. Donald G. Truhlar '65
2010	Dr. Jane Weydert Homeyer '86
2009	Judge Thomas L. Kilbride '78
2008	Edward J. Zabrocki, Jr. '63
2007	Joseph J. Ross '67
2006	Philip E. Corcoran '76
	Charles S. Wolande '76
2005	Patrick A. Salvi '75
2004	Michael O. Johanns '71
2003	Dr. R. W. A. Davidson '53
2002	Robert H. Wheeler '67
2001	Robert K. Hentzen '57
2000	Dr. Charles Giammona, Jr. '70
1999	Brother Andrew Benjamin Gonzalez, FSC '59
1998	Dr. Jon J. Kabara '48
1997	John A. Ehlert '67
1996	George J. Murtaugh '61
1995	David B. Collins '70
1994	Dr. Hugo C. Pribor '49
1993	John M. Sharkey '53
1992	Brother Leonard Courtney, FSC '37
1991	Carl J. Calabrese '41
1990	Edward M. Allen '50
1989	Anthony J. Adducci '59
1988	Thomas J. Johnston '43
1987	Thomas C. Barger '30
	Kenneth E. Wakefield '42
1986	Eugene E. Figliulo '46
1985	Dr. Lorin I. Nevling, Jr. '52
1984	Bernard H. Semler '38
1983	Thomas F. Meagher '53
1982	John C. Parmer '50
1981	Brother Laurence Walther, FSC '44
1979	Dr. Joseph R. Kraft '43
1978	Judge Michael A. Bilandic '47
1977	Most Reverend George H. Speltz, DD '33
1976	Dr. John H. Hoffman '51
	Dr. Robert A. Hoffman '56
1975	Judge C. Bernard Carey '56
1974	General John J. Hennessey '42
1973	Dr. John A. Sbarbaro '58
1972	Dr. William Rock '49
1971	Dr. Hugo A. Keim '56
1970	Dr. John Kearney '55
1969	Father Paul F. Halloran '49
1968	James J. Carroll '53
1967	Father Sylvester F. Brown '52
1966	Thomas J. Mulvaney '59

Photo by Florence Curran; Courtesy of Rob Linden.